A Field Guide
to PossibilityLand:
Possibility Therapy Methods

Bill O'Hanlon
Sandy Beadle

BT Press
17 Avenue Mansions, Finchley Road, London NW3 7AX

First published in the UK
April 1996

Reprinted with corrections
April 1997

Reprinted May 2000

Published by BT Press
17 Avenue Mansions, Finchley Road, London NW3 7AX
0171 794 4495

ISBN 1 871697 70 0

This is for Steffanie, who guided me into a whole new set of possibilities. My soul thanks you from the bottom of its little heart. And to my sister Suzanne, who always believed in my possibilities.

And this is for Bill Bronson, who saw the possibilities.

Acknowledgements

We would like to thank:
Doug Hagley for his invaluable support in graphic design, book construction, botany, and random moments of panic,
Dotty Decker, Mickey Price and Pat Hudson for help with early versions of the text,
Mary Nathan for handling all the details and keeping us organized.
Bill's clients, students and supervisees (thanks, I'm a slow learner, sometimes, but I'm trainable.)
And all of you who helped make this possible– you know who you are, sometimes.

Contents

A Field Guide to PossibilityLand

Preface to the UK Edition

This book by Bill O'Hanlon and his collaborator Sandy Beadle has all the characteristics of a Bill workshop. We are given 51 Possibility Therapy methods and are invited to experiment. The methods themselves range widely but, underlying each, we the readers will find a distillation of his ideas and a consistent set of values. We find it in the assertion that it is the client who will decide on the goal of therapy, in the authors' refusal to 'blame' the client for not changing and in their recognition that 'every client is an exception'. We find the authors' belief in clients, particularly in their resources and their capacity to change. We find acknowledgement not only of the potential of therapy but also recognition of the importance of ensuring that, as therapists, we do nothing that will make the problem harder for the client to resolve.

For the therapist the Field Guide is a challenge. A challenge to our assumptions - why do we do what we do? A challenge to our therapeutic habits - how would it be to introduce something new and different into our work? And as with Bill's clients we feel tempted to try to do precisely that.

Bill O'Hanlon is an exceptional workshop presenter. His presentations challenge and inspire. They are full of humour, lightness of touch while at the same time respect for the client runs right through. Bill's workshops are full of thoroughly practical ideas.

Above all the Field Guide is an inspiration.

Evan George
London, March 1996.

Front Words

Welcome to PossibilityLand!

We want to tell you some stories about this book, this therapy, and some interesting things that are in progress.

First of all, this book is about Possibility Therapy, in case you wondered. You will learn more about it as we go on, but briefly, this kind of therapy offers:

- Tested, practical methods.

- A new, more future and action-oriented approach.

- A way of encouraging both therapist and client to try new things and new ways to experiment with what works for the client.

- And an invitation to stay close to real life and out of abstract theory land.

Why this book looks so weird

What do you get when you cross a psychotherapy book with a guide to North American flowers, birds, and kitchen appliances? Ummm. . . Healing flights of fancy cooking? One good tern desserts another?

Well, we hope you get some useful and enjoyable information from our weird collaboration! And really, this jamming together of two wildly different book styles is not just an accident- we actually have a plan!

Some of the saner reasoning behind all this:
1. We wanted to break up a mass of information into small

chunks to make it easier to distinguish and remember and use as a reference. For that reason, it is set up in a method-by-method fashion.

2. We wanted to use humor to make a book about doing psychotherapy more friendly and approachable than is typically the case.

3. Because we wanted to design it in such a way as to make it easier for the therapist to do small trial runs, experiments, and explorations, to find out what works for a particular client.

The chapters are very roughly organized in the sequence of a therapy session, in this sense: methods we might use toward the beginning of typical sessions (and no, there is no such thing as a typical session) are in the earlier chapters, and those more often used toward the end appear in later chapters.

How this kind of psychotherapy came to be

Bill: I want to tell you a story about how I got started in this business and this philosophy. I got here through a very personal route. In 1971, I decided to kill myself. Now that may seem like a strange introduction to a guidebook that's designed to inspire you, but it's where it all began for me. I was very depressed and lonely at the time. I saw no possibilities for the future, aside from a continuance of the misery of the past. I considered myself a "poet" and certainly didn't want to work for a living. I was disillusioned by the hypocrisy I saw in society and in the people I knew. I felt as if I was all exposed nerves, as if I had no skin to protect me from the pain of the world and from contact with others. After a long and miserable time, I finally decided that I'd kill myself.

I was a hippie at the time and the few friends I went to say my good-byes to understood and accepted my decision. They would see me in another life, another time around the wheel, too bad it didn't work out this time.

One of my friends, however, got very upset when she heard my suicide plans. When I told her that the problem was that I just couldn't handle dealing with people and earning a living, she told me that she had some maiden aunts who were due to leave her some farmland in Nebraska when they died. She promised I could live in a farmhouse on her land rent-free the rest of my life, if I would promise not to kill myself. Now, that seemed like a possibility to me. "How old are your aunts?" I asked. When I heard they were in their sixties, I agreed not to kill myself. I was young enough that I thought someone in their sixties was bound to go soon.

Now I had a future I could live for, and the challenge was figuring out how to live and be less miserable in the meantime. I spent those years studying and learning, and feeling steadily better. As it turned out, those aunts, who were of solid Nebraska farm stock, lived for many more years- I never did get to take my friend up on her side of the bargain, because by the time she inherited the farm I was already happy and successful.

I now have a great marriage, a nice family with four kids, a successful career doing something I love, and a good income. Some of what I discovered on that journey from misery and suicidal depression to happiness and success is encapsulated in this guide. Over the years, especially when I was taught by Milton Erickson, I had the opportunity to study what actually worked in psychotherapy, and I have become passionate about spreading the word that there is a route from misery to happiness, from frustration to success. I call that route Possibility Therapy.

How this book came to be

Sandy: I am interested in the psychology of human information processing, how people learn and change, and how to make the process easier. My thinking in this has been influenced from three rather different directions. I've long been intrigued by Milton Erickson's work (and Bateson's and Haley's ideas about it.) I especially wondered how he could help people make such big changes with such small interventions. But I have also seen how difficult it was for people to learn his style of therapy, how people sometimes even resort to a kind of mysticism— like wearing purple clothes, as if some of the magic would rub off on them. I suspected there might be a better way of teaching this stuff.

The second influence has been my background in biology. I've taken a lot of science courses, and was really impressed by the way Voss, Wagner, and Barnes of The University of Michigan teach botany and ecology. They take a large and complex subject matter, organize it into distinct conceptual "objects," often creating visual representations, then show the relationship between those objects. I wondered if this way of organizing and presenting information could be used to help understand and teach other subjects.

Third, I've been studying how humans process information, with a special interest in how different media can help, and my advisor, Dr. Stephen Kaplan, taught me some key ideas:

- We learn more easily from bite-sized pieces of information organized in small clumps, and not just long strings of text (like this introduction!)

- Vivid and concrete images and visual cues help.

- It helps to exaggerate the key parts, eliminate the less important, and relate them to things people already know and are good at.

- A clear and visible organization, or ideas presented in story form, can help people to understand and remember.

- We can benefit by putting ideas in a usable and testable form, so people can begin their own small experiments.

When I met Bill O'Hanlon, he was in the process of de-mystifying Erickson's ideas (not that we have anything against the mystical!) and making them easier to learn in his workshops and training sessions. In addition, he had gathered a number of therapeutic ideas from other sources, and put them together in a very action-oriented way. After watching several of his workshops and talking with therapists who were trying to take these ideas back home and use them, I realized that the weeks after the workshop were especially important - when people went home full of energy, tried out a lot of things, had some success, hit some snags, then tried to figure out what to do next. I wondered if some of these techniques from very different, but perhaps oddly analogous, fields might be a worthwhile supplement to his workshops. I have been using computers as one way to put it all together, so I talked with Bill about making a computerized interactive video of a therapy session that people could take home after a workshop, so they could practice and learn the ideas more thoroughly on their own time. I wanted to organize it around individual methods as the "objects" that people could remember. Bill was pretty excited about it, so we got going, and in the process we started to write the text to go along with the video.

As we did, my scientific training kicked in, and I started to press him on a number of details: Is this method the same as that? How is this method related to the other one? What are some concrete examples of that? And as we talked, not only did the methods themselves become better articulated for both of us, so did their relationships, and hence their timing and uses. In the past, only by going through long apprenticeships could people really learn all three. We hope to facilitate that process, so that:

- Therapists can learn this material more easily.

- Therapists can pick and choose what is right for their practice.

- Therapists can more easily come up with their own novel solutions, which can be added to this growing body of new therapeutic ideas.

It also became clear that we had enough new and different material so that doing a separate text publication would be worthwhile. So we began the long and complex process of putting together a book. Bill developed the model, Sandy facilitated the articulation of the model, and used techniques of writing, organization and graphic design to increase the clarity and accessibility if the material. Sandy made Bill slow down long enough to explain what the hell he thought he was doing when he did therapy, and what this possibility stuff was all about. On the one day the two of us were actually in the same town, he paced around the room like a caged lion (being unwilling to take lithium or ritalin for his mania) and outlined a structure, while Sandy took notes furiously. Sandy then grabbed the computer and escaped to the woods, put the ideas into more coherent form, and designed what we hope will be a user-friendly format. Sandy prodded Bill out of his usual procrastination ("I don't like to write," says Bill, "but I like to have written.") Bill distracted Sandy from the depths of homework - a terrible, awful, horrible thing to do to a graduate student! ("I love writing," Sandy says, "but I'm not sure about this collaboration stuff yet.") And via e-mail and telephones and airports and conference centers and direct mental beaming, we put this crazy thing together.

And yes, the interactive video is still in progress. Now that we have organized the methods, we can get back to the grunt-work of teaching a computer how to put it all together for you.

The kind of therapy we are doing

In our view, therapy is about helping people reconnect with the sense of hope and possibility they have lost due to their suffering and pain. Unfortunately, as often as not, therapy has become a place where people hear things that discourage them: "You have a chronic mental illness and will need to be on this medication for the rest of your life," or worse yet, get blamed by the people they seek help from: "You are resistant," or "They don't really want to change; they want to hold on to their symptoms."

On the other hand, therapy can be so hopeful that it invalidates and alienates clients! Many naturally hopeful therapists have often avoided theories of pathology, preferring a more "positive" theoretical stance. Unfortunately, this positive stance can sometimes invalidate clients by accident, in this way - clients may have worked hard to construct sets of ideas to give meaning or dignity to their suffering - these can include hard-won self-labels, such as "co-dependent," or "ADD," or even a conviction that they are impossible to help - because no therapist in the past has been able to help them!

We have learned not to argue with that. We agree, and offer alternatives, and ways to move into and test out these alternatives. Possibility therapy is about acknowledging and validating clients' felt experience and ideas about their lives, while ensuring that possibilities for change are discovered and amplified. This approach attempts to introduce flexibility into the theories and methods therapists have, as well as introducing possibilities into the closed-down or self-blaming ideas clients have about themselves or their circumstances.

Iatrogenic injury and iatrogenic healing

Sometimes therapists don't know their own strength, and can do inadvertent damage. This happens when we turn something into a problem that the client was already handling successfully in some way. Or when we indicate that people are fixed, unchangeable, permanently typecast, or in other ways close down possibilities for change. Or while trying to change somebody's mind for the better, we invalidate them or show disrespect. Or when our interventions convince clients that we, not they, are the experts in their own lives!

Iatrogenic injury refers to problems caused by treatment, the result of the interventions done by the healing agent. It was initially applied to medicine, but has come to be used in psychotherapy as well. In 1961, Milton Erickson discussed the importance of this issue. "While I have read a number of articles on this subject of iatrogenic disease, and have heard many discussions about it, there is one topic on which I haven't seen much written about and that is iatrogenic health. Iatrogenic health is a most important consideration - much more important than iatrogenic disease."

Things that produce iatrogenic injury in therapy include methods, assessment procedures, explanations, or interventions that harm, discourage, invalidate, show disrespect, or close down the possibilities for change.

Iatrogenic healing is promoted by methods, assessment procedures, explanations and interventions that encourage, are respectful, and open up the possibilities for change.

That sounds pretty good to us. But even better, how about client-o-genic healing! No, it's not some fancy kitchen aid. It's a confidence that there are a number of ways we can help clients can find the resources they need to help in their own healing.

This guidebook includes a number of tips to keep us from sliding into iatrogenic injury, and help put iatrogenic and any other kinds of o-genic health and healing we can find into practice!

Why on earth did you put that there? The book's organization

This book is divided into five major parts:
* Acknowledgment and Possibility
* Change the Viewing
* Problems and Goals
* Resources
* Change the Doing

Bill: These chapters roughly follow the order of the things I do during the course of a typical therapy conversation (but, as we said, in real life, no session is typical.) Of course, mostly the things I do are all glommed together, but I separate them out to talk about them. Most of the time in the therapy session, I'm not thinking of these things at all, but am intensely engaged in the conversation. Like anyone who is absorbed deeply in something, I don't think. I just do. But to teach something, pulling it apart can be useful.

1. Acknowledgment and Possibility
That we begin with acknowledgment may seem fairly straightforward, but the kind of acknowledgment we advocate is unusual, and is one of the keys to doing effective therapy. Whenever we get the message from the client that we are not understanding or moving too fast, we make sure we acknowledge. We monitor both verbally and nonverbally to ensure that clients are feeling heard and validated.

The model that we have of therapy is like curling. Have you ever heard of the sport curling? You play it on ice. The teammates have brooms. Someone throws this big stone and players sweep in front of it to help it slide on the ice.

Like those curlers, we are going to be sweeping right in front the people we work with in therapy - sweeping open possibilities. And if we're going to sweep anywhere near the stone, we'd better pay attention to where the stone is right now, not where we think it should be. Translated into therapy-land, that means we'd better pay more attention to where clients actually are than to our theory about where they should be.

If our theory is focused on the present, but our client is oriented to the past, it is important to guide our attention to their past, at least initially. If we don't, our client is apt to feel misunderstood and invalidated and therapy can slide to a screeching halt. So we'd better go back and sweep right in front of them and say, "Yeah, that's okay, you can go back to the past." Validate that and support them when they're back in the past, and then start sweeping a clearer path into the present or the future.

We are big on introducing hope into therapy, but telling some people that there is hope can actually be invalidating. Have you ever tried this? Some people may spend most of their session telling us, "There is no hope!" And we're just as adamantly telling them, "There's hope! There's hope!" This is obviously not the way to run a baseball team! Instead of just trying to convince them that they're wrong, we can first acknowledge their rightness, maybe even explore the virtues of various cynical or fatalistic approaches to life. Or we can even ignore hope altogether, and go for some dumb little changes that can make a difference. We are not too proud to use anything we think will help!

If we keep sweeping where our clients aren't, we won't go far. They may keep telling us, and showing us, how sick and crazy they are, and how they really have to do this particular thing, and showing us that we're minimizing a really big problem. Or they may go find someone else who understands them!

Our way around this dilemma is to acknowledge in such a way that we validate clients where they are now without imposing our theories on them, and without giving in to the hopelessness of the situation. You'll find methods of doing this in this manual.

2. Change the Viewing

By "viewing," we mean what the client and others in the problem situation are attending to and what sense they make of it all. After acknowledging each person and their feelings and points of view, we offer many opportunities for all concerned to attend to different aspects of the situation, and to come to new conclusions or explanations about what has happened and what might happen in the future. We are already doing this when we acknowledge, but we carry it on throughout the therapy conversation.

This is more than "reframing" (in which the therapist gives a new interpretation to the problem). It involves the continual curiosity of the therapist and the co-creation of new perspectives. We frequently offer possibilities and ask curiosity questions. We make sure we do this in a way that gives clients the message that they can (and should) correct us if we are off-base. In our view, clients are the ultimate experts about their own lives and their experiences. They constantly teach us what fits and what doesn't.

3. Problems and goals

If you don't know where you're going, you'll probably get there! To prevent such a bewildering result, and to be appropriately client-driven, we are very concerned with getting clear conceptions of where to focus our change efforts. We want to be clear about how we'll know when we're getting there, and know when it is time to end therapy because it has been successful!

We're reminded of the funny prayer when the minister is blessing a battle in Mel Brooks movie, "Blazing Saddles,"

"Dear Lord, is what we're doing here today really important,
or are we just jerking off?" We are committed to the idea that
therapy is more than just jerking off, (not that we're against
jerking off generally, but you know what we mean) it is a
purposeful conversation that is supposed to do something -
relieve the suffering that people came in complaining about!

4. Resources
People may or may not always have the resources necessary
to make the changes they want, but they can be helped to find
them. We'd rather start with that assumption and let it be
proven wrong than starting with assumptions of inability and
deficits. That's because our clients often helpfully validate
our theories and assumptions! Sometimes we may have to
search the past for resources, or search areas not affected by
the problem, and sometimes we may have to look to social or
environmental resources. It helps to be resourceful!

5. Change the doing
Ultimately, if therapy is to make a difference in people's lives,
it must have an influence on their actions. We focus on
getting a description of the actions (the "doing") involved in
the problem, we try to identify any patterns in those actions,
and then take specific steps to help the person change those
actions and patterns.

How to approach this guidebook

We suggest that you look over the guide, pick out two or three
specific methods you find interesting, and give them a try. See
how they work with your current clients. It may also be
worthwhile to tell clients you are trying something new that
they may find useful. Then, when these become automatic, go
back and pick a few more.

Above all, lighten up. Therapy always involves on-the-job
training, and is a lifetime learning process. And there's no need
to live your life in drudgery! Look for what works, do small
trial runs, test out new ways of thinking and acting, and don't
be afraid to have fun with it, to laugh and see the lighter side.

We encourage you to take an experimental and humorous approach to therapy. Remember that if you fall on your face, at least you are headed forward. Maybe seeing you do this will encourage your clients to do the same! Perhaps we will be able to recognize Possibility Therapy clients by the scuff marks on their noses.

And remember, this is all made up. That doesn't mean it's not true or useful. Just that it's made up. When it comes to helping real live people, there are few eternal verities, and lots of useful territory to explore. We hope our delusions will prove helpful to you and your clients, and that you will soon be contributing your own.

We want your help with this - please send us your ideas and comments about what works in this book, and what you would like to see in the next edition.

Chapter 1
Carl Rogers with a Twist

Acceptance and change. Acceptance and change. Remember
these three words, because they are the essential components of
therapy. Like Carl Rogers, we accept people where they are
right now, and help them accept themselves. But then we add a
little twist. We communicate, "where you are now is a valid
place to be, AND you can change." Then, using a variety of
skillful means, we help them do just that.

Clients will signal us if we push the change part too hard or too
fast - they act "resistant," unhappy, or tell us that we don't
understand, or they go find someone else who will listen to
them more respectfully.

If we push the acceptance part too far, and don't get on with the
change, they may wallow or stay stuck. They may feel heard
and understood, but often they don't change. We want to
provide enough acknowledgment to support and validate
clients to make the changes that they came for. To accomplish
this balancing act, we use what we call possibility language.

Possibility language involves a number of different ways of
using language to break up and rearrange what the client knows
in order to facilitate change. How we speak about ourselves and
our lives can influence feelings in subtle and profound ways.
Small changes in our repeating mental talk can make a big
cumulative difference in how we feel and, even, to a certain
extent, how we act. In this chapter we present a number of
carefully designed ways to use language to help open new
possibilities.

It's important to acknowledge and accept clients where they are
right now, but that's often not enough to make a permanent
difference. In addition, clients are helped to see that they
actually can make changes, get a taste of how life feels after the
difficulty is resolved, and look for specific steps they can take to
get where they want to go.

1.1 Possibility-laced acknowledgment

Definition **Possibility-laced acknowledgment-** Let clients know that you have heard and understood their suffering, their concerns, their felt - experience and their points of view, without closing down the possibilities for change. The simple fact of not arguing or invalidating what the client says is a form of acknowledgment. But any kind of acknowledgment is only half of the job. Acknowledge AND keep the possibilities open.

Rationale This typically takes three forms:
1. Reflect back what the client has said or shown in the past tense.
2. Reflect global statements as partial statements.
3. Reflect a "truth" or "reality" claim as a perception.

Examples *Client:* I'm totally depressed.
Therapist: So you've really been down. ("Been down" instead of "are down" is an example of reflection using the past tense.)

Client: I fail at everything.
Therapist: So you've failed at most of the things you've tried. ("Most" instead of "everything" is an example of reflection moving from global to partial.)

Client: He hates me.
Therapist: You've really gotten the sense that he hates you. ("Gotten the sense" instead of claiming it's the whole truth and nothing but the truth that he hates the client is an example of reflection of truth-statement as perception.)

1.2   *Escalator language*

Definition   **The Moving Walkway -** Acknowledge while leading your clients to a view that a future they would prefer is possible, and that they are already heading towards such a future. Like a moving sidewalk in an airport, these techniques move clients along in the direction of possibilities without them actually taking steps toward their goals.

Rationale   This method is similar to possibility-laced acknowledgment, except that this time the therapist leads a lot more, introducing future possibilities while acknowledging current concerns and experience. Again, just to be symmetrical about it, how about three methods for this:
1. When clients speak of the problem, reflect in a way that states their concerns as preferred goals rather than problems to be gotten rid of.
2. When reflecting, summarizing or clarifying, use words that convey an expectancy that the preferred future will come about.
3. Reflect with the addition of words like "yet" or "so far" to suggest that sometime in the future, the problem will end or things will be better.

Examples   *Client:*   I feel hopeless and lost and don't know what to do.
Therapist: So you'd really like to get a sense of hope back in your life.

Client: We're fighting all the time.
Therapist: So we'll know we're successful here when you are getting along a lot better most of the time.

Client: I can't seem to keep a relationship going.
Therapist: So far you haven't sustained a relationship as long as you'd like.

1.3   *Read the feedback*

Definition **Read the feedback -** Watch for ongoing verbal and nonverbal feedback, and use it to guide your moves.

Rationale Feedback is our richest source of information.   Ernie Rossi, a Jungian analyst who studied with Milton Erickson, tells of how Erickson constantly had to redirect Rossi's attention to the client. Erickson would often look over and notice that Rossi was looking at the ceiling, spinning theories and having conversations with himself about what was going on. Erickson would remind him that there was no client on the ceiling - the client was sitting across from him. So, instead of having conversations with your theories or looking at your theories during therapy, it's important to look at clients and have conversations with them. They have a lot to teach you!

If the client seems to act "resistant," disagrees, doesn't cooperate, gets quiet, or tunes out, this valuable feedback often indicates that the change-part is being pushed too fast or hard, and it's time for more acknowledgment. This is how clients let you know how things are going, and what does and doesn't work for them. Sensitivity to such messages can save both therapist and client time, confusion, and discomfort. And since we have many methods, we don't feel discouraged when something we're doing doesn't work or fit for the client - we just try something else.

Examples *Client:*   No way! I will not talk to her!
Therapist: OK, not a good plan. Would you maybe talk to your brother, or write a letter, or not communicate with her at all yet, or...?

Client: You don't understand me!
Therapist: OK, I'll try to understand better. Can you tell me what I've said to give you the sense I didn't understand?

Client: (Silence)
Therapist: Um, it's gotten pretty quiet in here, so I may have to make some guesses, maybe that (watching closely) you're feeling pretty discouraged, or misunderstood, or that this is going too fast, or - (client responds) oh, going too fast? OK.

1.4   *Match language*

Definition   **Match language -** Participate in verbal patterns by matching language. Use similar words and phrases, speed, or intonation to join with the client and lay the foundation for later change.

Rationale   Language matching can be a very subtle and powerful way to show others we are on the same wavelength. The phrase "We speak the same language" evokes this experience. And we don't use jargon that distances us from clients - unless it's their jargon! Erickson was a genius at language-matching - once he even went to the trouble to learn word-salad so he could communicate with someone who spoke it exclusively, and in the process helped the man to change. Remember not to use this or any other as a manipulative technique, but instead as a respectful way of joining in your clients' worlds and not making them come to yours.

Examples   *Client:* I'm a miserable dumb stupid fool.
Therapist: So you've been feeling like a stupid fool lately.

Client: Well, you know, I kinda don't know, well, I just, ah, I don't know.
Therapist: Well, I don't know, but I wonder if it was kinda hard to talk about it when you felt like that.

Client: Maybe I'm not meant to be happy until my next lifetime.
Therapist: Why are you on the planet this time around, do you think?

1.5   *Utilization*

Definition   Utilization - Take what the client brings, no matter how small or odd or even negative the behaviour or idea seems, and use it to get the person moving again.

Rationale   Erickson taught us that the therapist can take whatever clients bring and use it to help turn their lives around. Anything, a skill, a symptom, even a lack of response may be used as leverage in therapy. For example, we might use a client's obsessive patterns to get him to obsess about what he's going to do with his life once he's over his symptoms.

This method has a number of effects:
• The therapist values and includes whatever the client shows or brings to therapy as part of the change process.
• Nothing needs to be "wasted"- there's no such thing as a weed, as the rock group The Move sang some years ago.
• The client is now seen as providing valuable resources.
• And even the oddest or scariest symptom is seen as a source of hope and possibility.

This contrasts with the more pathology-focused approaches, which see many things clients bring as symptoms or liabilities.

Examples   *Client:*   All he does is listen to heavy metal music all day, and he's too dumb to learn anything.
Therapist: (to the son) What are some of your favourite song lyrics?

Client: My life is nothing. I can't even leave the house. All I do is talk on the phone.
Therapist: Have you ever thought about getting a job that you could do from home on the phone?

Client: I'm a failure. I mess up everything I do.
Therapist: I've got a weird suggestion for you then. For the next week, I'd like you to deliberately fail at five things, and give yourself permission to fail. If you succeed at failing, you'll be able to get some experience at success, and if you fail at failing, you'll obviously succeed. It's a win-win proposition . . . Unless you screw it up, of course.

1.6   *Inclusion*

Definition **Inclusion -** Include any parts, objections, feelings, aspects of the person, or the person's concerns that might have been left out, or seen as barriers to the therapy or goals.

Rationale Along with the utilization approach, in which we use everything that might help, we also include anything that seems to have been left out, or devalued, or seen as irreconcilable opposites. Sometimes we think of this as the big AND (as opposed to, in Pee Wee Herman's immortal words, the big BUT.) Our clients give us ideas or feelings that seem to be in opposition—BUTS, and we reflect them back as ANDS.

Examples *Client:*   I am afraid to tell you about my abuse, but I think it is really important.
Therapist: You can be afraid and tell me, and you don't have to tell me until you are ready.

Client: Maybe I'd be better off just being celibate, given the trouble I get in with romantic and sexual relationships.
Therapist: Maybe you would be better off, and maybe we can find a way to help those relationships go better.

Client: I want to end it all. I can't stand the suffering one more day.
Therapist: You can feel desperate and want to kill yourself, and you can stay alive.

1.7   *Include objections*

Definition **Include objections** - Include and accept objections the client makes as valuable feedback, which may also indicate that it's time to do more acknowledging.

Rationale Objections, like "resistance," are seen as sources of crucial information. If clients say it's not working, it's not right, or it's not what they want, the therapist can modify the approach, and perhaps do more acknowledging. Then we offer multiple choices, change tenses, or try other options from this magical therapeutic bag of tricks.

Examples *Client:* No, I know that will never happen.
Therapist: OK. I guess I need a clearer idea of what you want.

Client: But I can't do that!
Therapist: So right now you're pretty sure you can't do that.

Client: When I tell you about my problems, you always seem to focus on positives. I'm not sure you understand how bad it is for me.
Therapist: I'm sorry, but sometimes I get psychotically optimistic. I keep hallucinating your future with things working out. Maybe someday they'll invent a medication to help me with my problem, but until then, if I get too optimistic, please remind me and I'll try to adjust.

1.8   *Include opposites*

Definition **Include opposites** - Never forget the dark side, the hidden side, or just the other side, and include it so it won't become a booby trap for either therapist or client.

Rationale We don't believe that people have some dark, seething, unconscious inner volcano ready to erupt. But we do know that if some part of life is too strongly denied, it may try to make itself heard elsewhere. This is fairly easy to deal with - just make sure nobody is trying to hold to one side of an issue too strongly.

Examples *Client:*   So do you think that I've finally overcome my drinking problem for good?
Therapist: Well, you either have or you haven't. Time will tell.

Client: I have to talk about the abuse I suffered, but I just can't.
Therapist: You may be able to find a way to tell me and not tell me. Or you can feel afraid to tell me and tell me anyway.

Client: I just want to quit my job sometimes.
Therapist: One time in graduate school, after getting a busywork assignment from one of my least favorite teachers, I got disgusted and felt like quitting. I just felt stuck. As I walked out of class, I went by a wastebasket and realized that I could drop my books in the trash and never come back to class. With that settled, I thought about it and redecided that it was worth all the hassle to get my degree. It was important to acknowledge that I didn't want to do the busywork and I wanted to get the degree, and that I had a choice.

1.9 Validate, value, & hold accountable

Definition Validate, value, and hold people accountable for their actions -
Validate and value clients' being and inner experience, while
still holding them accountable for their actions.

Rationale Thinking does not mean acting. Feeling does not mean acting.
What we experience inside, what we think and feel, no matter
how strange, are OK. What we say and do are another matter.
Certain things we say or do can hurt people, lead to trouble, or
just keep the problem going. Those behaviours are what we
need to change. Finding out whose fault something was or who
was to blame often don't matter; changing things does.

It's important to hold people accountable for their actions
without blaming them. You can make it clear that they took the
action, and that it's their choice, without suggesting that they
are bad, or evil, or had bad intentions.

Example *Client:* It's all my fault. I wrecked the friendship.
Therapist: Well, it usually takes two to tango. What do you
think was your part in damaging the relationship?

Client: She just nags and nags until she finally gets me to hit
her.
Therapist: So you've hit her and have had the idea that she
provokes you into it. Tell me about some time when she
provoked you, but you kept yourself in check.

Client: This eating thing just comes over me and I can't control
myself.
Therapist: Next time you feel like that, what will be your first
cue to act differently?

1.10   Give permission

Definition   **Give permission for being** - Let the client know it is OK to have automatic experiences such as sensations, involuntary thoughts, feelings, and images.

Rationale   Controlling actions is possible, but trying to control thoughts or feelings is difficult. Blaming people for their thoughts or feelings is counterproductive. The first step in changing our experience is to accept where we are right now, quit fighting with ourselves, and move on.

We usually give permission for inner experience in two forms: permission to and permission not to have to. Some people are stuck on one side of the equation - they think they are terrible for having some experience or thought or that they shouldn't think or experience it. Those people need the permission to experience or be something. ("It's okay to think about killing yourself. Many people have thoughts like that.") Normalizing is one way to validate and give permission. Once clients hear that others have the experience, they don't feel so abnormal or weird.

The other side of the equation is that some people are stuck with an experience that dominates their inner life. Or someone has told them that they should be having some experience that they are not having. They might need the permission not to have to have the experience. ("You don't have to remember the abuse if it's not right for you.")

Examples   *Client:*   I'm a lesbian and I keep having these sexual fantasies about men. My best friend says the fantasies are just remnants of my sexist, homophobic conditioning, but I kind of enjoy them.
Therapist: It's okay to fantasize about having sex with men. You probably spent a lot of time coming to accept your lesbian desires and not make yourself wrong for having them. Why let your friend shame you for these fantasies?

Client: Oh, no, I see it all again, she's coming at me with the knife, she's - oh no, no -

Therapist: Just go with it, just let it happen, I'm right here, you can keep talking and let it flow right on past until it's done.

Client: I never got angry after my husband died. I read a book that said anger is one of the stages of grief. Do you think that there is something wrong with me?

Therapist: Everyone goes through grief in their own particular ways. I don't think the author of the book meant you have to go through those stages, only that many people do.

1.11   *Decline invitations to blame*

Definition   **Decline invitations to dwell upon hopelessness or blame -** Let the client's invitations to blame himself or others pass in silence, and focus on invitations for hope and possibilities.

Rationale   Blame tends to focus people in the past where no action is possible, and where people more easily get stuck. Even worse, it is often impossible to state with total certainty who was to blame for a given event, particularly in long-term relationships. So you might never even be able to find out "who is to blame!" Focusing on what is wanted and needed in the future, and on desired outcomes, is both more reasonable and more useful. This is not the same as denial or non-accountability. We still want to acknowledge what happened to the person and who took action in the situation. What we mean by blame is attributing bad intentions or qualities to people instead of describing what the person did.

Examples   *Client:*   My mother beat me repeatedly before I moved out.
Therapist: She abused you a lot. How, in the face of that abuse, did you develop the courage to move?

Client: I feel terrible, because now my children are becoming Adult Children of Alcoholics and I've ruined their lives, just like my father ruined mine.
Therapist: Maybe they can benefit from your experience in dealing with your father. How will you advise them so they can avoid some of the pitfalls you have suffered?

Client: How could I ever turn out OK with what happened to me?
Therapist: I don't know, you seem contrary enough that you might do very well.

Chapter 2
CHANGE THE VIEWING

"A problem is an opportunity in drag."
Paul Hawken, *Growing a Business*

Introduction

We believe that therapeutic and personal reality is socially influenced. That is, concerns which bring people into therapy aren't set in stone, but rather are negotiated in language and by attention. This is what we call the VIEWING of the difficulty, (and we prefer to talk about difficulties rather than problems. When we remember.) The viewing is what people pay attention to, including frames of reference, perceptions, explanations, and predictions. The therapist helps the client shift ideas that close down possibilities, and draws upon ideas and experiences which indicate that positive change is possible, and often already underway.

Included in this chapter are four kinds of discouraging or disrespectful explanations that we steer away from, and help clients change:

1. Explanations that blame clients for their problems (remember that by blame we mean attribution of bad intentions and traits, not holding people accountable for their actions.)

2. Explanations that invalidate clients experiences.

3. Explanations that preclude the possibilities for change.

4. Explanations that remove or block the recognition of personal accountability.

In addition, we help clients reorient their attention to things that help them move on rather than things that keep them stuck or discouraged. One such reorientation is to help people notice, articulate and highlight times when they were problem-free or did better despite their difficulties. This is part of the method and philosophy called "solution-oriented therapy," of which possibility therapy is a descendant.

We also typically orient the client and his or her intimates away from a view of the client as pathological and towards a view that the client is competent and resourceful.

We like to "normalize" what is going on with people as much as possible without trivializing or minimizing. Part of this involves using simple language whenever possible, avoiding jargon or psychiatric terms, except where really necessary, or where we think it will help make a point more memorable. We consider everyday speech valid and helpful. Old-fashioned and colloquial words can encompass the range of human difficulties while keeping us firmly grounded in common sense. And when used without minimizing or disrespect, these words often provide a better basis for change. It's easier to help a client who wants to stop worrying about whether someone is trying to control her if she wears certain colors than it is to treat a "paranoid schizophrenic." It is easier to help parents whose daughter has stopped eating than parents whose daughter has the disease of anorexia. It makes more common sense to help someone who often disregards his needs in favour of others than to cure "codependency."

"Nothing is as dangerous as an idea when it is the only one you have."
Emile Chartier

2.1   *Use humour*

"In therapy, you are very careful to use humour, because your patients bring in enough grief, and they don't need all that grief and sorrow. You better get them into a more pleasant frame of mind right away." Milton H. Erickson

Definition **Use humour**- Use humour or anything that gets clients to see their situation as less grim, without disrespecting or minimizing their pain and suffering.

Rationale Humour can be used sensitively to lighten up distressing situations, help equalize client and therapist, and assist the process of change by rearranging mental associations. The mere fact of coming in for therapy can intimidate clients. Humour can help de-mystify and lighten the process of therapy, and give clients a taste of the more enjoyable experiences they are seeking. Humor is also itself a powerful change agent - we all know of a joke that has made us see things differently.

Despite rumours to the contrary, even the most serious therapists are allowed to use everything from small word-twists to slapstick, to help clients build the lives they want. Take care that the client is sufficiently acknowledged and that you are not making any put-down jokes, then let your zany or whimsical view of the world make a difference.

Examples *Client:*   I'm just so depressed.
Therapist: So how long have you been living in Depresso-Land?

Client: Um, you know, she didn't quite, well, do it, you know, um, on time.
Therapist: Um, can you be a little bit more vague?

Client: Are there any microphones hidden in here?
Therapist: As a matter of fact, the local public radio station is doing a fund-raiser and asked me if they could broadcast a session with my most paranoid client during pledge week. I forgot to mention it, but you're on now. Could you give them this pledge number? 599-6111. Thanks.

2.2   *Assume times without problem*

Definition **Assume past and present problem-free times -** Ask and talk
about problem-free times, even if they only occurred while the
person was unconscious!

Rationale There is almost always some time and situation where a given
difficulty didn't occur. Find it, and inquire in detail about it,
asking what, when, and with whom it occurred. Then use the
facts, feelings, and ideas associated with these times to build
new plans and successes.

Examples *Client:* I just can't seem to get up in the morning.
Therapist: Didn't you tell me that you had to milk the cows
when you lived on the farm? How did you get up so early
when you felt like lingering in bed then?

Client: The thoughts just keep circling.
Therapist: Is it better at night, or in the morning, or in the
evening, or at work?

Client: I sure wish I could stop smoking.
Therapist: How do you keep from smoking while you are in a
movie?

Client: He's been schizophrenic for so many years that it's hard
to remember he was ever normal.
Therapist: So your son has been schizophrenic since he was
nineteen. What can you tell me about the times of lucidity since
he started having the hallucinations?

2.3   *Assume client is active agent*

Definition Assume the person is an active agent in his or her life -
Suggest that any success was a result of the client's efforts.

Rationale Clients, when they are feeling bad, can blame everyone for their
successes except themselves. Whenever possible, indicate that
the client was the one who took actions, no matter how small,
that had positive effects.

Examples *Client:* Then things just got better with us.
Therapist: Which of the things you said made the most
difference in things getting better?

Client: My last therapist saved my life.
Therapist: That's impressive! And how did she help get you to
the place where you decided to change?

Client: I feel really terrible.
Therapist: And feeling as terrible as you do, what did you say
to yourself to get up this morning to come here?

In response to any report of worthwhile things occurring, ask
about the client's power or the choices made in the situation.

Client: Then things started going really well at work.
Therapist: How did you get that to happen?

Client: I felt totally hopeless when I first lost my job.
Therapist: What did you do to get things back on track?

2.4   *Deframe*

Definition   **Deframe** - Challenge and introduce doubt into old beliefs that aren't helping.

Rationale   Sometimes people have been considering situations in a way that doesn't work. We gently challenge their ideas and frames of reference about those situations, without necessarily adding new ideas or frames of reference.

We don't think that clients' ideas are rigid, unchangeable structures that exist within them. To us, they're more like houses of sugar cubes that got crystallized by the conversations and interactions that have gone on with others and with oneself. We help decrystalize the client's house of sugar cubes and their invalidating rigid structures by challenging various unworkable frames of reference, including:

- self-blame - "I'm just totally worthless."

- Unchangeable self images - "I can't change because I'm a schizophrenic."

- Invalidation - not trusting one's own sense or perception of thing - "I don't feel attracted to him because that would be a sin." "I'm too messed up to know what I like." "I can't tell if he's mean or I'm too sensitive."

Examples   *Client:*   I guess I'm just selfish.
Therapist: Is it more that you are selfish, or maybe you just like to take care of yourself?

Client: The doctor said I have a depressive personality.
Therapist: Oh boy, that means we get to do a personality transplant!

Client: I'm a stupid no good fool.
Therapist: Then what makes you think you are qualified to judge yourself so harshly?

2.5   *Use action descriptions not labels*

Definition   **Depathologize by moving from reifications to action descriptions -** If an experience has become thing-like, divide it back up into a process, a sequence of mental and physical actions.

Rationale   Reification is when we turn a process - "I go to bed and then it takes me three hours to get to sleep," into a thing- "My insomnia." The therapist can help turn that noun back into a process. "My insomnia" is a big gray immovable lump that's hard to change, but "I go to bed and start thinking about problems and get all riled up," can suggest modifications of actions and habits to bring about the desired change.

Examples   *Client:*   I've been depressed for several months now.
Therapist: So there have been a lot of times lately when you felt just plain lousy.

Client: These panic attacks are driving me crazy!
Therapist: When you have what you call a panic attack, what do you notice first?

Client: He wants to be independent, but it makes me feel left out.
Therapist: What does he do when he does things that he calls independent?

2.6   Depathologize by changing labels

Definition **Depathologize by changing labels -** Change devaluing or pathological labels to more everyday, amiable, more change-available ways of talking about difficulties.

Rationale   Most of us know that it isn't particularly therapeutic to let someone call themselves a "rat-faced loser," so we acknowledge it as how they might have felt, and go about changing the label. But it's still a fairly new discovery that such labels as "obsessive" or "borderline" may be just as devaluing and harmful to the client, of little use in treatment, and actually limit the therapist's effectiveness.

People have gone a bit label-crazy these days. Even kids from the finest families are subject to "I-want-to-go-play-rather-than-mow-the-lawn" disorder, as though almost everything is an illness, perhaps because it sounds rather impressive. But life is complex, and people do things for all sorts of reasons, or no reason at all. Treating normal human thinking and behaviour as illnesses can make everyday difficulties harder to untangle, change, and move beyond. We take these events and behaviours out of the operating room and put them back in real life where individuals can make a difference.

We normalize, destigmatize, and depathologize by indicating that others have similar experiences, renaming patterns of actions, and changing labels we stick on people.

Examples *Client:*   He's a vicious monster.
Therapist: Well, let's try to break that down - what exactly does he do that bothers you?

Client: But everybody knows that borderlines can't form relationships.
Therapist: Maybe you hadn't heard - due to the new inclusive language, "borderlines" are now known as "interfaces," and that changes everything.

Client: But I'm an Adult Child of an Alcoholic.
Therapist: Oh no - do you realize what the next stage is? You become an Adult Adolescent of an Alcoholic!

2.7 *Frame difficulty as a stage*

Definition   Depathologize by framing the difficulty as a stage - Speak about the problem or concern as a developmental stage, something that the person might grow out of or get over.

Rationale There are many ways that people change, and one of the most familiar is how they change as they move from childhood to adulthood. The therapist can use this in two ways - first, with clients who might not recognize that a given difficulty is common to a particular developmental or transitional stage (the honeymoon is over, new kid on the block, not having sex much after the first child is born, etc.) Second, this can be used as a metaphor for things less typically developmental, but which can usefully be seen in such terms.

Examples

Client: My daughter is a failure - 26 and she still doesn't have a husband or a career.
Therapist: I was a really late bloomer too, but I finally got it together in my late 20's.

Client :   I can't concentrate and I don't want to go out and I don't even know what I'm interested in anymore.
Therapist: Sounds like you have a serious case of graduate-student-itis.

Client: I don't even know what I'm doing with him.
Therapist: Were your friends too polite to warn you about the post-honeymoon letdown?

2.8   *Beat them to the punch*

Definition **Depathologize by beating them to the punch** - Before clients
even have the opportunity to fully describe the problem, beat
them to the punch by describing it in a less pathological and
more solution-oriented way.

Rationale This helps in several ways:

- It shows the client that you understand.

- It lets you establish a more workable definition right from the
  start.

- And it lets you start with an intervention.

Watch for the feedback on this, so that when you are wrong, and
you will be wrong at times, you can make corrections quickly.

Examples *Client:*   But then, after everything that happened yesterday -
Therapist: You stayed awake worrying when you would
normally have been asleep?

Client: Then my son came home with a terrible report card,
and my mother refused to call my sister back, and then the dog
caught a skunk, and my anxiety -
Therapist: - got the best of you for a while. How did you finally
calm down again?

Client: Well, at first I was flying.
Therapist: But, of course, that high right after the session wore
off.

2.9   *Normalize*

Definition   **Normalize -** Speak about the concern as if it is in the realm of normal human experience, rather than an exotic or terrible thing.

Rationale   Sometimes people come to therapy thinking that they are crazy, going crazy, or are like aliens with no connection to human beings. Normalizing can help get them back in the human race, so they feel they are more okay and perhaps maybe actually can be helped! Even more severe problems can be normalized, such as the relatively common problems of bulimia or self-mutilation. Once clients know that we know about the problem, that we don't think they are sub-humans or weird aliens, they often already feel a bit better by just being connected with other people again.

Examples   *Client:*   I feel as if everyone knows I was abused.
Therapist: Yes, some people who've been abused do have that feeling.

Client: I think about suicide sometimes.
Therapist: Actually, I have considered suicide in the past, and most people I've talked to in my counseling have at one time or another thought about it. Did you been seriously considering doing yourself in or did you made specific plans recently?

Client: We're having a rough time being a blended family. The kids resent him as my new husband.
Therapist: Maybe you expected there to be instant intimacy or closeness, or you hoped things would gel more quickly. Most people find they have "lumpy" families for quite a while before they get blended.

2.10 *Split & Link*

Definition **Split & Link** - Use words and gestures to help the client make distinctions, breaking up old limiting or unpleasant associations and habits, and linking things in new ways with more potential.

Rationale In a general sense, splitting and linking are the building blocks of how we make sense of the world. We make certain distinctions (splitting) and certain associations (linking). Many of the methods we discuss involve this mechanism of mental change, in which old thoughts, habits, expectations and patterns are broken up, and new patterns form. Using both words and gestures, we help make new distinctions and new associations that open possibilities.

Examples *Client:* I feel awful because Laverne didn't say a word, so he must be mad at me.
Therapist: Do you think he was quiet because he was mad at you, or maybe he was feeling down, or maybe he was just thinking about his day?

Client: I felt so terrible yesterday.
Therapist: OK, now, I want to know which days you felt terrible, and which days you didn't.

Client: I enjoyed my sexual abuse.
Therapist: Do you mean you felt physical pleasure but didn't want to be intruded upon, or did you like the experience because you were too young to know that it was inappropriate and intrusive, or that you actually liked it?

2.11   *Externalize the problem*

Definition **Externalize the problem** - Put the problem outside the client by personifying it, or seeing it as a set of behaviours, so it can be grappled with more easily.

Rationale When the problem is seen as all inside a person, or worse yet, as a built-in part of the person, it can seem much harder to change. But a difficulty that is externalized, even jokingly, becomes more removed and easier to deal with.

Examples *Client:*   I'm just a depressed person.
Therapist: It must be tough, living in Depresso-land.

Client: I'm always scared.
Therapist: So tell me about those times when you face up to the fear monster.

Client: I'm ugly and stupid.
Therapist: When I was young, I had a Howard Cosell voice in my head that gave me a critical running commentary on everything I did wrong. What does your Howard Cosell voice tell you to try and convince you that you are ugly and stupid?

2.12   Use metaphors and stories

Definition **Use metaphors and stories** - Metaphors and stories are indirect ways to communicate ideas. They involve talking about something that parallels or represents something else.

Rationale We use stories to instruct, show steps to be taken, give good examples, and help normalize. People enjoy and easily remember metaphors and stories. Bill had a friend once who went through five years of psychoanalysis. Because her analyst spoke rarely, the only things she actually remembers of what he said during the five years are three stories he told at critical junctures in her treatment. Pretty powerful stuff, these stories. We use them to give clients a tool kit of reassuring, encouraging, and inspiring images that are easy to remember. A story can provide a powerful array of images. And a metaphor, even the silliest cliche, may help someone see things in a new light.

Stories can include actual experiences and discoveries of real people, including other clients, friends, or famous people. They can include stories heard or seen, or myths, fables and fiction, if they are identified as such. Although some therapists advocate making up "real-life stories" and then present them to the client as if they really happened, this seems a bit disrespectful to us, and may cause unwanted confusion or distrust.

Examples *Client:* I just feel so broken up inside.
Therapist: Like any self-healing system, your inner ecology will be seeking its own natural balance.

Client: I'm a failure, I sleep until noon every day and miss classes.
Therapist: When I was in college I was an expert at not getting up in the morning. I had it down to a science.

Client: After this blowup with Marge, I can't go on.
Therapist: Sometimes a blowup clears the air, or sometimes you just have to accept your losses.

2.13   *Provide new frames of reference*

Definition **Provide new frames of reference -** Use what the client brings, but offer a new point of view or interpretation, often of the same material which has just been deframed.

Rationale Take the raw material, the sugar solution, and recrystallize it into a new rock candy. Agree with and retain a given set of facts, but put them in a different context. This is an especially nice technique because it draws upon and organizes some of the wealth of experience each client brings to therapy.

Changes in framing can include:

- More useful alternate views that fit the facts of the situation
- Changes in explanations and evaluations, or stories
- Attribution of different intentions, traits, thoughts, feelings, and experiences.
- New labels and names.

Examples *Client:*   I always see the worst side of everything.
Therapist: Now wait, you just told me you weren't sure whether he was leading you on or not. It seems to me like you look at both sides, and you try to keep a balanced view.

Client: It's terrible - I weigh 250 pounds!
Therapist: So there are times when you've bought into the cultural idea that people have to be at a certain weight or look a certain way to be acceptable?

Client: My brother says I just can't seem to hang on to my money.
Therapist: So you spend the money you get pretty quickly and your brother thinks it's important to hang onto money? Does that reflect a sense of abundance, like somehow, some way you knew you would always have enough to get by?

Chapter 3
MAP PROBLEM AND GOALS

Perhaps you are wondering why we put such a basic chapter way in here instead of at the beginning. Did you think we just forgot? Actually, there are several reasons, but a major one concerns emphasis. This kind of therapy is not directionless by any means, but it isn't exclusively goal-driven either. In this kind of therapy, we are so interested in focusing on possibilities and solutions that we may extensively open up possibilities and validate the client before we have a clear focus for the session or the therapy. It is not only possible, but often useful to get these acknowledgment and change steps in motion before we even know the problem or goals.

This odd state of affairs can occur because our focus is to help clients find out what they are good at, and focus on what is going well and on how to move into the lives they want, rather than focusing solely on symptoms, and then treating the symptoms. The difficulty our clients brought in may be resolved, or they may find out they have the resources needed to solve it, or they may see they aren't "sick" or "crazy" as they feared before they came to see us. Or they may decide it was really not such an important issue after all. We consider any of these outcomes a success!

On the other hand, it is easier for a therapy to get lost if the goals are not clear. If we find ourselves getting bogged down, we use goal-finding and goal-setting methods, then move back to acknowledgment and change.

Well-formed goals consist of actions clients can take, or conditions that can be brought about by clients' actions. Often they include time elements:

- How often (frequency)
- When (date/time/deadline)
- How long (duration)

The goal can be defined in terms of:

1. Resolving the concern that brought the client into therapy or

2. Recognizing when enough progress has been made so we can stop therapy or take a break from therapy.

The goal must be mutual. If there is more than one client, or the customer (the person who initiated therapy and is motivated to making things change) is not the client, all parties must agree that the goal is relevant and achievable.

Sometimes it is important to inform clients that you are searching for an achievable goal and give them a rationale for your search. For example:

1: "I keep going back to this issue of how we'll know when we've been successful and can stop meeting, because I want to make sure we're working on your goals, not mine."

2: "I am concerned that what we're doing in here could become (or has become) part of the problem instead of the solution. I think defining a goal will help avoid that, because we'll have a clearly identified stopping place."

3: "Sometimes therapy becomes a slippery business. It's like nailing jello to a tree. It can be discouraging wondering whether I'm really helping people change, or just passing the time. So pinning down a specific goal would help me out."

But it is also possible and useful and - yes - even permitted, to begin therapy with goal-talk, right off the bat. We focus on the goal and a successful outcome as early as we can without alienating the client. If we get messages that the client is irritated with the focus on goals, we either explain our purpose, or back off and refocus on what they indicate is more important to discuss. The following is an actual example of how to use goal-talk in the first minutes of therapy:

"This may seem a funny place to start, but I always like to know where I'm going, so I can listen better for what will be helpful to you. So, if you can, tell me what you hope will be happening in your life when we've been successful in here. What will you be doing after therapy? How will others know you've changed?

How will you know? And if you can, I'd like to hear it in a way that I can imagine seeing on a videotape."

A reminder about language: We find it very helpful to use words like complaint, difficulty, concern, and not problem. But we make sure we are not disqualifying clients when we use this language! And we indicate that the issues are taken seriously. If the client thinks it's a problem and it would seem minimizing to hear these alternative words, go ahead and use the 'p' word.

3.1   *Specify goals*

Definition **Negotiate with the client to specify achievable goals -**
Negotiate achievable goals in videotalk, in terms of actions or
results that could be seen and heard on a videotape.

Rationale During times of stress, clients can easily lose sight of what
matters, so it can be useful to formulate clear, concrete goals.
This helps focus both client and therapist.   Getting specific
helps us check if the goals are realistic, and later, if they have
been met. This is an important stage in therapy, as we believe
that clients come in with ideas and concerns, and through
conversation, shaping and checking it out, we collaborate in
creating a focus for therapy. Like a chess game, the opening
moves define the possible moves in the game. This is an
important point for opening up possibilities for solutions.

Sometimes we help clients take goals from the ideal down to the
practical by asking about interim goals, or steps to
accomplishing the goal.

Examples *Client:*   He's got such an attitude.
Therapist: So when he has a better attitude, how will you be
able to tell? What are some of the things he will say or do that
will show you that change?

Client: I'm going to get off drugs.
Therapist: That's a pretty big goal. In order to move in that
direction, what would you need to do in the next week?

Client: I want to quit messing up.
Therapist: So tell me how it will look when you quit messing
up? What will a typical day be like?

3.2   *Specify the complaint*

Definition Specify the complaint - If the complaint seems unclear to either client or therapist, have the client briefly describe it in videotalk.

Rationale Have clients say in videotalk exactly what the difficulty sounds like, looks like, or what they are thinking as it is happening. Once this is clear, move the focus to how things will be when the complaint is resolved, so client and therapist don't get stuck in problem-land.

If you clarify and specify the goal, it will usually help you understand the complaint. If you clarify the complaint, the goal becomes focused.

Examples *Client:*   Richard is not behaving, and I'm at my wit's end.
Therapist: OK, when you say he's not behaving, I need specific examples of that in order to understand what you mean. What exactly does he say and do?

Client: He's just a hopeless psychotic.
Therapist: What are some of the things he says that give you that idea?

Client: I'm just miserable all the time.
Therapist: That sounds pretty bad. But be more specific, what does feeling miserable involve? What do you think, how do you act when you are miserable, as opposed to when you're feeling better?

3.3   *Specify achievable goals*

Definition **Specify achievable goals -** Go into detail about goals, making sure they are reachable, preferably by the client's efforts.

Ask questions to clarify goals, create strong images of the desired actions and results, and reinforce the assumption that success will occur. Two questions are especially useful:
"How will we know when we get there?"
"How will we know when we are finished?"

Rationale As we define goals and sub-goals, we also need to make sure they are what the client wants, not some stray idea that has crept in during the course of therapy!

Example *Client:*   OK, I'm supposed to call her and apologize before I take the job?
Therapist: Now, just to make sure we are still on track, is this job what you really want?

Client: I want my marriage to be perfect.
Therapist: OK, can we bring that more into reality-land - and be a bit less vague? What are some specific things that will indicate it has improved?

Client: I want to make her love me.
Therapist: Ummm ... well, if I had a love potion, I could really make money! But I don't, so let's keep it within my skill-level. Which actions would you expect her to do more as she loves you more?

3.4   *Quantify vague goals*

Definition **Quantify vague or "feeling" complaints and goals -** Have clients rate or scale their concerns, suffering or unpleasant feelings. Then have them tell you where they would be on the scale when the problem is resolved or therapy has been successful.

Rationale Obviously we prefer to translate vague words and phrases into action-based language. Goals are more checkable if clients state them as if they could be viewed and heard on a videotape player. Sometimes, however, people are loathe to describe their concerns or goals in action-based terms. It feels false or forced to them. If the therapist insists, the client may feel misheard or misunderstood. Instead, have the client quantify, scale, or rate the subjective experience of the problem and the desired feeling or state that would indicate success. Then find action steps the client could do that would improve the rating to the desired level.

Example *Client:*   I don't know what I'd be doing when I'm feeling better about myself. It's not something I do, it's inside.
Therapist: On a scale of 1 to 100, where would you rate your current or recent feelings of self-esteem and where will it be on that scale when you have reached your therapy goal successfully?

Client: I want my marriage to improve.
Therapist: Okay, that's a little vague for me - what percentage of time do you think your marriage is okay now, and how much would it have to improve for you to get the sense it's where you would like it to be?

Client: I'm good at pretending. No one else knows I'm depressed.
Therapist: What has been your level of depression on a scale of 1-10, 0 being the most depressed you've been?
Client: A five.
Therapist: Okay, what do you think you could do that would help raise that to a level of six over the next week?

3.5   *Find sub-goals*

Definition **Find sub-goals -** It can sometimes be helpful to agree to clear sub-goals, and highlight intermediate landmarks that will indicate signs of progress on the path to the goal.

Rationale Most of us are encouraged by little rewards along the way, little feedback signs that we are on the right track. For one thing, it makes our work more manageable by breaking down a big task into parts. Second, distinctive signs also encourage us to look for the next landmark, to "keep our eyes on the prize," or at least looking toward it. This means the focus changes from "can I do it?" to "what is the next sign that I AM doing it?"

Examples *Client:*   I want to find a good relationship.
Therapist: Okay, time to plot out a strategy! What can you do first?

Client: I am going to write that damn dissertation!
Therapist: Okay, a good goal, but this is a pretty big bite all at once, so let's break it up into several parts.

Client: I feel fragmented.
Therapist: What will be the first sign that you are coming together?

3.6   *Use multiple choice*

Definition **Use multiple choice questions and statements -** Offer multiple choice questions, yet another form of guiding question, which can seed new ideas while gathering information.

Rationale Provide multiple choice options when clients hesitate in stating clear goals, or when they continue to answer your queries about their goals with vague words and phrases. Sensitivity to verbal and nonverbal cues will help you use this method to its greatest potential. When we offer each choice, we are carefully watching the person for his or her response. Some people, especially kids, may have trouble putting complex feelings and ideas into words, and repeated multiple choice questions give them an opportunity to make themselves understood. Remember that ideas can be contagious, and the multiple options you provide will likely influence how your clients conceptualize their concerns and their goals.

Examples *Client:*   I don't feel so good.
Therapist: Does that mean that you've been unhappy emotionally, or you've got some medical problem, or you aren't happy with the things you are doing?

Client: I kinda do this. (Pulls hair)
Therapist: So when have you typically pulled at your hair? At night? Or when you've been alone? Or while watching television? Or when you have been tired?

Client: I don't know anything about women.
Therapist: Now do you mean you're not sure how to start a conversation with a woman, how to approach them sexually, or how they'd like you to ask them for dates?

3.7   *Use magic wand questions*

Definition   **Use magic wand questions -** Ask questions that orient the client to a future in which things work out, without having to stop and figure out specifically how to get to that future.

Rationale   Magic wand questions help us do a number of things:

- Clarify and focus on goals.

- Create strong images of doing preferred actions.

- Create the assumption that success will occur.

- Help us find the juice, the powerful interests and images that pull the client along.

From there, of course, it is often a matter of working backwards from that ideal future, to action steps that might create such a future. Sometimes, however, just getting the client clear on the goal can pull them towards that future without specifying exactly how they will get there.

Examples   *Client:*   I don't know what to do with my daughter.
Therapist: Imagine a miracle, so that things suddenly worked out between the two of you - give me the details on how that would be.

Client: School isn't right, my job isn't right, my relationships aren't right, and I don't know what to do.
Therapist: Well, let's pretend for a moment. What if your wildest dreams could come true, and everything suddenly worked out beautifully, what would you be doing?

Client: I sure wish I could get back to my art.
Therapist: If we could wave a magic wand, and your creativity was flowing, what kinds of artistic things would you be doing or producing?

3.8   *Presuppose goal achievement*

Definition **Presuppose that the goal will be achieved -** Assume that therapy will be successful. Use words like "will," "when," and "yet," when speaking about clients' therapy goals and post-therapy goals.

Rationale Erickson once said that if his client needed to go into the psychiatric hospital, he would always discuss what they would be working on after the person got out of the hospital, in order to reassure the client that he or she would indeed be getting out! He would presuppose getting out of the hospital. In a similar vein, we want to presuppose that clients will reach their goals. Remember that language is a virus, and it is likely if you presuppose success, your clients will be infected with your confidence regarding their goal achievement.

Examples *Client:*   I'm too afraid to approach women.
Therapist: So you haven't asked a woman out for a date yet and you'd like to be able to get into a relationship?

Client: I'd like to get out of this depression.
Therapist: When you're feeling better, less depressed or not depressed, you'll be getting up earlier and spending more time with friends?

Client: I sure wish I could get back to my writing.
Therapist: When you are writing more, will that be an indication that things are going in the right direction?

3.9   *Avoid symptom-talk*

Definition **Use everyday language, not problem-talk, to describe the concern and the goal** - We avoid medical jargon and prefer commonly used words in our therapeutic conversations. This can help to bring both clients and ourselves out of the mumbo-jumbo of symptom-talk and back into the everyday realm of thoughts and feelings and actions.

Rationale When we use words like "difficulties", "concerns" and "feeling down", it might seem like we only deal with rather minor problems. But we use such language even for people who are suffering under such diagnoses as anorexia, schizophrenia, and involutional depression (that's some scary sounding language, isn't it?) We intentionally put even severe difficulties into regular non-medical everyday language, to bring the most frightening and uncontrollable-seeming experiences out of the mystical medical realm, back into the human world of actions and changes and choices.

While we in no way want to minimize the client's pain or treat serious things less seriously, this way of speaking highlights that each individual is unique, exceptional, and is far more than a diagnostic category. And each client has unique experiences, resources, and ways of resolving the difficulties they come up against.

Examples *Client:* He's schizophrenic so he's impossible to be around.
Therapist: Sounds like his schizophrenic times were worse the last few weeks. What's made the crazy times different from regular times with him?

Client: The doctor said he had Hyperkinesis with Attention Deficit Disorder, and I don't know what to do.
Therapist: Well, since you probably haven't had time to learn medical Latin, we might start with a translation - in plain English, the doctor said he jumps around a lot and doesn't pay attention as much as most kids.

Client: My doctor said I have functional impotence and he sent me to you!
Therapist: So when was the last time you got hard?

3.10   Go for directions and trends

Definition **Go for directions and trends rather than goals -** If goal-talk ·
seems too strong, we ask clients whether some of the things that
have been happening are a trend they would like to have
continue, of if things they say they want are a direction they'd
like to pursue.

Rationale Sometimes goals may seem forced, or the client is upset when
we purse goal questions too much. Since our purpose is to find
what is relevant and useful to our clients, we'll settle for an
imprecise formulation of trends or direction rather than specific
goals. Most clients don't precisely specify goals at the beginning
of therapy, unless they are trained in goal-setting, or are
engineers or software programmers!

Examples *Client:*   I've been enjoying our marriage lately.
Therapist: Is this a good direction for us to focus on in our work
together then, increasing your enjoyment in your marriage?

Client: I've gained a few pounds.
Therapist: I know that has freaked you out in the past, when
you were in the grips of Anorexia. Is that trend okay for you
now, though?

Client: Part of me is afraid you'll kill me, and part of me trusts
you and knows that's crazy.
Therapist: So we'll know we're making progress when the trust
is stronger and the fear is fading?

Chapter 4
CONNECT WITH INTERNAL AND EXTERNAL RESOURCES

We have this weird idea that our clients are very resourceful, that they have resources within themselves, as well as in their surroundings that can help them resolve their concerns and reach their goals. In one of Carlos Castaneda's books, he was studying with the Yacqui teacher Don Juan, who kept sending Castaneda on adventures in the desert to meet his "allies, " spirits that attempt to trick and kill Castaneda. He always managed, however, to defeat these spirits, even though he had many close calls. After one particularly gruelling night battle, Castaneda wandered back to Don Juan's house and complained that he had again almost been killed by one of his allies. He asked Don Juan why the allies were getting stronger and more clever. Don Juan replied that the allies were always matched perfectly to Castaneda's strength. They were no stronger or weaker than he is, so the outcome of the struggle was not predetermined. "You are never sent any allies that you are not capable of defeating, since they are always matched to your own strength. As you get stronger, the allies that confront you are also getting stronger. It's a good sign when more powerful allies begin to appear. When you defeat an ally, its strength enters you and becomes a part of you."

We think this way about clients. They are never confronted with difficulties that are beyond their resources. Those resources can be personal, interpersonal or spiritual.

Now this may be a strange or perhaps naively optimistic idea, but don't tell our clients! They always seem to show resourcefulness. So we either have an elite group of people coming into our offices, or just maybe people are influenced by what we expect of them.

The methods in this section are designed to connect clients with their own resources, skills, opportunities, and different ways of thinking. We help them find and focus on resources that they have previously demonstrated, and also seek out resources that are available in the people and the community around them.

4.1   *Evoke an experience of resourcefulness*

Definition **Evoke an experience of resourcefulness -** Use examples from the client's own history to evoke the inner experience of resourcefulness.

Rationale When someone is feeling bad, the things they have available and are good at don't always leap immediately to mind! The therapist can come prepared with a set of questions to elicit past times of competence, skill, and hope. We ask clients to go into detail about things they have actually done and felt, even if these seem currently unrelated at to the issue at hand.

It's important to not only remind clients of things they are good at and enjoy, but to help them connect with the emotional experience of these resources by asking detailed questions about skills, accomplishments, and their confidence and satisfaction in things they have done. This way they can show us that they are or have been resourceful and competent, rather than us trying to convince them of it!

Examples *Client:*   But what can I do? I've never even been on a date!
Therapist: Let's look at when you've had enjoyable times with other people. Tell me more about how you talk to your close friends and how you first got to know them.

Client: I'm having trouble in school, and my mum yells at me, so I just go to my room and read comics. I get so into them, I end up not doing my homework.
Therapist: So you are likely to spend a lot of time reading comics when things aren't going well for you. Tell me what you like about the comics.

Client: The other girls at school just laugh at me because I look different.
Therapist: I hear that you have several pen pals - how have you gotten to be friends with them?

4.2   *Find choice-points*

Definition   **Find choice-points** - Ask or talk in detail about choice-points and change-times, times when the client made a choice or a change for the better. Then explore similar points of opportunity in the present and future.

Rationale   Times when the client made even the smallest change for the better can suggest places to intervene. So can times when the client made changes for the worse! Either type of change can tell us about things that break up the pattern of the problem, and help us pinpoint places for our interventions.

The interesting thing is that even very small changes in the doing or viewing of the problem can make a difference. These can make change-images more available and put things back in the client's control.

Examples   *Client:* Things are really stuck with my husband.
Therapist: You told me that things were bad in the first year of your marriage too. How did you come out of that bad time? What made the difference?

Client: Well, it isn't quite as bad this week.
Therapist: What the first sign you noticed that the pain was getting better?

Client: Yeah, I have been writing some - three pages, actually.
Therapist: You wrote three pages this week - what got you going on that?

4.3   *Find times without the problem*

Definition   **Times without the problem** - Examine in detail how the client felt and acted when the current difficulty did not occur, even just for a moment.

Rationale   When we have enough time, we humans can think about a multitude of things, but at any given moment our "channel capacity" is limited. This limit obviously causes us some difficulties, but also has a number of advantages. For example, if we can keep several strong, hopeful, enjoyable, engaging things in mind, we will have less room left over to focus on what's gone wrong. This "limit" also'helps us keep focused and keep moving.

When we have clients recall times without the problem, we:

- Help them fill their minds with images and associations of things going well.

- Reconnect with the skills used then.

- And perhaps set in motion some of the mental and emotional patterns that have worked previously.

Examples   *Client:* We've been fighting a lot lately.
Therapist: What do you like to do when you two aren't fighting?

Client: Well, I pretty much feel hopeless, except for that strange week after the accident.
Therapist: Well now, that's interesting. Tell me more about that week.

Client: Right now it's just me and my honkey-tonk records.
Therapist: Sounds like you are sort of lonely now. Have there been some times recently when you felt alone but weren't really lonely?

4.4   *Find exceptions to problem*

Definition **Find exceptions to problem -** Look for times when the problem was expected, but something happened differently or the client acted differently.

Rationale There are almost always exceptions to a given problem:

- Times when it doesn't happen.

- When it doesn't happen the same way.

- Or when there is a different response to it, even if it is only when the client is asleep.

Such times can become gateways to longer and longer periods of time when the client is free of the difficulty.

Examples *Client:* Yeah, except for last Sunday, forget it.
Therapist: But wait - last Sunday you spent the whole day with your mother without feeling guilty? How did you manage that?

Client: I can't control it, everything goes haywire and I freak out and nobody's safe.
Therapist: You said you never hurt the guitar that your cousin fixed up for you. What other things do you or could you protect even in the worst times?

Client: I guess it's not surprising I'm not too hungry then.
Therapist: So you stop thinking of food in the dentist's chair. That's a start.

4.5   *Find what worked*

Definition **Find what worked -** Get detailed descriptions of what has worked for the client in similar situations, or talk about what worked for other people with this difficulty.

Rationale It is not uncommon that clients have had a similar difficulty in the past and have successfully resolved it. The client might have simply forgotten the old solutions, not connected them with the current difficulty, think it might not work, or just need a little encouragement to try it again. Our work is a lot easier when we can find such examples from the past and use them now. We can help the client:

- Focus on what worked.

- Get details.

- Expand on details.

- Retrieve how it felt to have things work.

These are all important parts of possibility therapy, and things that distinguish it from the pathology focus. And, as we said before, when we are thinking about something that worked the way we wanted, focusing on it, musing about it, planning it, remembering how great it feels, talking about it, it's a lot easier to do that particular activity than if we are stuck in how awful things are, how awful we are, or how hard our past was.

Examples *Client:* I just can't get to bed at a reasonable time.
Therapist: Didn't you say that Mickey helped you with this a long time ago?

Client: What's wrong with me that I fight with my mom like this?
Therapist: You said your brother used to get in fights like this with your mom. How did he get out of that?

Client: It feels terrible, having this come back again.
Therapist: You said you saw a therapist for this once before. What did you and she do that worked?

4.6   *Find competence*

Definition **Find competence** - Find the client's areas of competence, interest, and pleasure, get the details of these, and highlight and expand them.

Rationale Everybody is good at something, even if it is a small thing, like a skill at washing dishes, or a "pathological" thing, like consistently feeling worthless despite outside influences! We find whatever we can, and use it.

We can help clients draw upon the confidence and ease they feel in situations (even in the "negative" examples) where they are competent and effective. They can also draw useful metaphors, strategies, sources of inspiration, and practical help from these areas, and apply them to current areas of difficulty.

Examples *Client:* I feel helpless to change his mind.
Therapist: Didn't you tell me that you were a great advertising person, very creative? How could you use some of that advertising creativity to change his mind?

Client: I just hang around all day, and the teachers say I'm not good for anything.
Therapist: Your mother says you are in a band. How did you get good enough at music to get into a band?

Client: I keep everyone away. No one can get close to me.
Therapist: So you are good at keeping yourself safe and isolated. How do you do that?

4.7   *Transfer competence*

Definition **Transfer competence across contexts** - Help the client transfer competence from another place in his or her life to the problem-area.

Rationale Obviously, this method is akin to the previous one, but here, instead of just finding and highlighting the person's competence, we help them apply that competence to the problem area. This can involve a direct transfer of skills, for example, when a salesperson uses her sales skills to help her son in school, or more metaphorically, when a skilled but shy outdoorsman considers how dating is like making one's way though the wilderness.

We highlight areas in which the client is competent and create bridges for the smooth transfer of the information. This can include using metaphors and making practical suggestions.

Examples *Client:* I've given up - nothing is working with Joan.
Therapist: How would a top executive like you save a business about to go bankrupt? How can you use those same skills in saving your marriage from bankruptcy?

Client: My mother and her brother squabble constantly.
Therapist: You run a daycare - when you see two kids fighting, how do you help them get along better?

Client: He'll never listen to me, and if I try to say something I'll just mess it up.
Therapist: You're good at writing- what if you wrote him a note about what you want?

4.8   *Who or what else can help?*

Definition **Who or what else can help?** - Directly ask about or suggest external resources.

Rationale Erickson was a master at finding resources in the community. He knew shopkeepers and kids and old people, people who had a variety of skills and interests, and would connect clients with them. Even if we do not live in such close-knit communities, there are still many ways the client can be introduced to useful resources. The simplest way is to ask the client who can help. It's also not against the rules to introduce clients to community resources or other people you know that might help them. Self-help groups are an obvious example, but there are many other resources you might use. Where would you go or who would you seek out if you faced a concern similar to that of your client? Answer that and it might give you a hint of what direction to suggest to the client.

Examples *Client:* I have to learn this biology stuff, and it makes no sense to me.
Therapist: Who do you know who's good at this who might help? Maybe you could barter with someone who needs their bike repaired, since you are a whiz at that.

Client: It just seems so lonely now that Shirley's gone.
Therapist: A friend of mine who was feeling isolated found it helpful to go to her local restaurant for breakfast every morning, just to have some familiar faces around. Laurel's Kitchen is a nice place, you ever tried it?

Client: I'll never find a boyfriend.
Therapist: When my daughter was frustrated about getting a boyfriend in high school, my wife suggested she carefully observe a friend of hers who was a great flirt and find out how she attracted boys. So, who do you know who's really great at finding boyfriends?

4.9   *How come it didn't get worse?*

Definition **How come it didn't get worse?** - Ask clients to explain to you what has restrained them from going further in their problem patterns.

Rationale Problems don't go on forever, and for most people, haven't gone so far as they could have. Asking about the limitations of a problem highlights for clients that they have some limits and control, and can give you hints about how they keep things from getting worse, another possible source of resources or solutions.

Examples *Client:*   I can't believe how much I weigh!
Therapist: How come you haven't gained more weight? I mean, I've known people who have gained more weight than you and I'm sure you know some people like that as well. So how do you keep yourself from weighing even more?

Client: I felt like hitting her again.
Therapist: How did you finally calm yourself down and stop the violence?

Client: I can't stop smoking pot.
Therapist: How come you never got into harder drugs?

4.10   *Find the stopping pattern*

Definition **Find the ending or stopping pattern** - Ask clients how they stopped the problem or what they started doing once it was going away or went away.

Rationale Sometimes we can't find good examples of exceptions or prior competence at finding solutions. Then we ask clients about:

- How the problem goes away.

- How they got out of it.

- How they stopped it.

- What they started doing when the problem eased up.

- What they started doing when the problem went away.

Often this gives us ideas about which actions under their control we might encourage.

Examples *Therapist:*   What do you do as the depression is lifting that you weren't doing much or at all when you were depressed?
Client: I start to go out of the house more, call my friends and start looking for a job.

Therapist: What things have you done that have helped the headache go away a bit quicker?
Client: Well, if I can get myself back to exercising regularly, even if I have to start slowly, they seem to go away sooner.

Therapist: How can you tell that he's about to stop throwing his tantrum?
Client: He starts to look up at me from the floor and he stops banging his fists.
Therapist: Then what do you do once you see those signs?
Client: I begin to talk more softly to him rather than yelling.

Chapter 5
CHANGE THE DOING

"We are not things, but patterns that persist."
Norbert Weiner

Introduction

In many cases, by the time we get to this part - changing the actions involved in the problem - we have actually done the majority of the therapy work. We have helped develop changes in how clients think, feel, and experience themselves, the world, and the difficulty that brought them to the office. This is quite a lot!

This is because we have already made a multitude of small interventions, which set the change process into motion. What remains is to map out and arrange for changes in specified patterns of behaviours. Once someone asked Bill at a conference, "So, do you think change in therapy occurs from things that happen within the session or things that happen outside the office?" And Bill answered, "Yes." (That's why we call him Mr. Inclusion!) This chapter is mostly about supporting and facilitating change outside the office. The pattern mapping and homework assignment methods in this chapter are particularly designed to continue the change process outside the session.

Because we often focus on how people act and what they say, we are sometimes accused of being behaviourists. Us, behaviourists? NOT!

Unlike behaviourists, we think there is a lot of crucial stuff going on inside people, stuff that has changed before, and will again. We know that changing thoughts, patterns of thinking, and experience can change how people act. But we also know that actions can change how people think and feel. And so can words, context, light, and brain chemistry. We are ready to intervene in any or all of these areas when it will help our clients get where they want to go! Behavioural theory is, for us, like any other theory - a point of view that may be useful in certain situations. It may just as likely be a hindrance in other situations.

We emphasize action because it is easy to track. It is also relatively easier than feelings or experience to change by direct effort. We are big on the idea that people are not set the way they are now, but do their lives in patterns - some neurological, some physiological, some cognitive, some attentional, some affective, some interpersonal, and some action patterns. Emphasizing the doing gives us lots of ideas about how and where to focus our change efforts.

5.1   *Map patterns*

Definition **Map patterns of actions -** We inquire in detail about the patterns related to the difficulty - how, where, when, and with whom the difficulty occurs.

Rationale In the same way we had the client "describe the difficulty in videotalk," we now examine, in videotalk, the pattern of actions and events that make up and surround the difficulty.

Most difficulties involve a sequence of thoughts and actions, and a set of contextual cues, all of which play a part in keeping the difficulty going. When we can find several points where we can intervene, rather than just one, we are much more likely to derail the difficulty and get the client back on track.

Examples *Client:*   Yeah, I want to work on the fighting part.
Therapist: So what did you do as the fight was starting - what was the first thing you said? Then what did he say? What room were you in? What time was it? Has it usually happened more at night?

Client: I don't know, the voices just come.
Therapist: So when the voices come it's usually after you've had an argument with your mother and you are back home alone?

Client: Yeah, it's getting to sleep that's the real problem.
Therapist: On the nights when you've had trouble getting to sleep, lets start a few hours before bedtime - what do you do to start getting ready?

5.2   *Compare and contrast*

Definition   **Compare and contrast** - Compare times when the difficulty occurs with when it does not occur, emphasizing actions under the client's control.

Rationale   This can be used very early in the session as a valuable way to simultaneously gather information, acknowledge the problem, and build stronger images of problem-free times. It is especially important to emphasize actions the client did, either verbal or nonverbal, not in order to blame, but to find pivot-points for change. Sometimes during this process, information emerges that would not emerge if one only asked about solutions or only asked about problems.

Examples   *Client:*   My depression is what I want to work on.
Therapist: So tell me about a typical day when you were depressed, the first thing you do in the morning, then compare that to a day when you are feeling better and less depressed.

Client: So I guess I just can't keep a job.
Therapist: You mentioned that you once kept a job all summer. Now I want you to compare that with this last job you didn't keep. What were the differences, what did you do in each situation?

Client: I hate this bingeing!
Therapist: What's different about the times you don't binge? Compare what you do on those days you don't binge and contrast it with the bingeing days.

5.3   *Pattern interventions*

Definition **Design pattern interventions** - Intervene in several of the small details of the way a problem pattern is played out, until you discover one that changes or eliminates the pattern.

Rationale Many small, cumulative interventions in a variety of places in a problem pattern can be a very effective way to bring about positive change. The client is less likely to object to small interventions, and more likely to be able to carry them out. And because many difficulties involve a sequence of repeating steps, using a number of interventions will offer more opportunities for clients to pop themselves out of their ruts.

One interesting and hopeful note is that sometimes, the more rigid and ingrained the problem pattern, the easier it can be to break up, because even one small change can throw the whole thing off!

Here are some suggestions as to how to change the pattern:
1. Change the frequency or rate of the complaint or the pattern around the complaint.
2. Change the duration of the complaint or the pattern around the complaint.
3. Change the time (hour/time of day, week, month or time of year) of the complaint or the pattern around the complaint.
4. Change the intensity of the complaint or pattern around the complaint.
5. Change some other invariant quality of the complaint or pattern around the complaint.
6. Change the sequence or order of events involved in or around the complaint.
7. Interrupt or otherwise prevent the occurrence of the complaint.
8. Add a new element to the complaint.
9. Break up any previously whole element of the complaint into smaller elements.
10. Have the person perform the complaint without the usual accompanying pattern around it.
11. Have the person perform the pattern around the complaint at a time when they are not having the complaint.

12. Reverse the direction of striving in the performance of the complaint [Paradox].
13. Link the occurrence of the complaint to another pattern that is a burdensome activity [Ordeal].
14. Change the body behavior or physical performance of the complaint.

Examples   *Client:*   Yes, setting the timer helped too.
Therapist: Okay, then how about, as soon as you notice the fight start, you set the timer for fifteen minutes and then sit on the floor until the timer goes off. If they ask, tell them every worker deserves a coffee break and you, as a mother, are taking yours.

Client: But what if I just binge again?
Therapist: OK, that will be the signal to try this out: Next time you feel like binge eating, take a shower, put on your makeup, put on your fanciest dress, and then you can binge if you still want to.

Client: I usually get so nervous that my voice and my hands start shaking.
Therapist: How about if you practice getting your voice and hands to shake when you're not giving a speech? That could give you more control over those things at the critical time when you need more control.

5.4   *Restore what worked*

Definition **Restore useful patterns that worked** - Search for things in the past that worked and have the person do those things again.

Rationale It's OK to use old solutions! Sometimes clients just forget to try what worked before. Sometimes they don't realize that an old solutions can be applied to new slightly different problems. Find things that worked before, link them to current difficulties, then specify which of the operations the client can apply now.

Examples *Client:*   I can't handle this crazy schedule.
Therapist: What if you went back to your old habit of getting up and swimming in the morning before work?

Client: I feel lonely and useless since Richard died.
Therapist: You said you used to go out with the Sierra Club. That might be one way to meet some new friends, and also do some good while you are sorting things out.

Client: I haven't been able to meet anyone since I graduated and moved here.
Therapist: How about taking some non-credit or credit classes here, since you met a lot of your old friends through classes?

5.5 *Action plan with homework*

Definition **Action plan with homework assignments -** Work together to plan specific actions for the client to take after the current session is over.

Rationale In this step, we put it all together. At this point, therapist and client can get very specific, agreeing to exact times, actions, things to say, and whatever will be most helpful. It may be useful to have the client practice some of these within the session.

It is important to check verbally and non-verbally to make sure that clients actually can and will do the things we agree to. This is definitely not a contest of wills, and there's no one right way to proceed. It is a simple contract we are negotiating to get things accomplished. If modifications are needed to reach the goals, we go right ahead and make them.

Examples *Client:* She's going to start complaining about her health again.

Therapist: Now when you talk with your mother on Tuesday, this time find any way you can to agree with almost everything she says, just as an experiment, and to get both of you into a different way of talking.

Client: My mother will be shocked if the bed is dry.
Therapist: Well, let's go for one dry bed between now and next time, just to cause a little excitement around the house.

Client: And if it happens again?
Therapist: OK, remember, if the auditory hallucinations return, you right away turn on your stereo headphones loud to Beatles music, and if the visual hallucinations come back this week, you will call your brother and take a walk outdoors for at least 20 minutes with him. Does that sound OK? And do-able?

5.6   *Relapse prevention*

Definition **Anticipate and plan relapse prevention -** Things don't always go smoothly in the course of making significant changes, and it's OK to let the client know this. Just make it clear that it is temporary, that the change part is what counts, and that things will soon get back on track.

Rationale The first trick in this method is to avoid self-fulfilling prophecies. We do that by assuming that things will work out well in the long run, and that some difficulties are a normal part of life and change. Within that frame, there are some common stumbling blocks clients can watch out for, so they can go around them, or catch themselves if they start to fall, and keep right on going. It is also important, at every stage, to make sure that clients are not setting up unrealistic expectations about things beyond their control - such as how another person might feel, or some event that might take place. Stick close to the client's own thoughts, feelings and actions, and it will work the best.

Examples *Client:* But what if I mess up?
Therapist: Oh, of course that sometimes happens, but it's just a normal phase in a change as significant as this. We're not going for perfection, only improvement.

Client: But what if I get into that depresso-thing again?
Therapist: Everybody has a down day now and then. Sometimes people make a quick trip back to depresso-land to pick up something they forgot, but you've shown that you've learned things that can get you a round-trip ticket back to where you want to go.

Client: Does this mean I'm cured?
Therapist: Hey, I'm not allowed to give away any happy endings before the last chapter is over.

5.7   *Know when to stop*

Definition **Know when to stop -** It's OK to end the session, or the therapy, as soon as you are done! We avoid the temptation to go over the difficulty again and again. When things click, and we know the client gets it, we stop right there!

Rationale This knowing-when-to-stop is another thing that gives this therapy its characteristic flavour. Fifty minutes is no magic number. Even a few minutes into the session, while the client's head is still spinning, the therapist may have already made a number of important interventions, and see that it's time to stop. This isn't a race, speed is not a goal, and it is especially not something to force upon the client, nor is there anything wrong with doing things rapidly. Make sure the client is satisfied and has the necessary closure. Just don't continue out of some misplaced convention, politeness, or because of what the clock says.

The therapist can be helpful in many ways other than regular sessions. Sometimes a phone call to check in is enough, or actually preferable, putting more of the responsibility and pride of accomplishment back with the client, as well as limiting expenses. Stopping by the office, or checking in with someone else may be what it takes. Sometimes letters or other forms of communication work even better. Monthly or irregular sessions can also be appropriate. Do what works for this particular client.

Examples *Client:*   Well, yeah, I guess I can do that.
Therapist: Well, OK then. How about if I expect you to stop by the office for a few minutes tomorrow morning at nine, and every morning for the rest of the week, just to check in?

Client: OK, I guess that's it.
Therapist: So, we've covered everything we need to for now? OK. See you in two weeks.

Client: You know, I've already made the changes I want, and it's only taken three weeks.

Therapist: Well, I've seen stranger things. Shall we call it a wrap? You can phone me if something else comes up.

"Psychotherapy is an undefined technique applied to unspecified cases with unpredictable results. For this technique, rigorous training is required."
– Raimy (1950)

Back words:
The next, but not final, frontier

The relationship of brief therapy to possibility therapy

Possibility therapy is generally brief, though not always. Brief therapy sometimes gets a bad rap as "a band-aid on a gaping wound." Therapists who are accustomed to doing longer-term therapy and who are not solution-based and goal-oriented can't image that brief courses of therapy can be respectful or effective. In this book, we have tried to show that they can be both. Another source of misunderstanding, which has been made much worse in this era of managed care and increased third-party scrutiny of therapists, is that many people get brief therapy mixed up with time-limited therapy.

Time-limited therapy is based on the idea that if the therapist or insurance company predetermines the number of sessions (usually 3 to 20 sessions), the therapy will be more efficient, because both therapist and client hunker down and get to work, knowing they have no time to spare.

While that approach has something going for it, it rests on different foundations than brief therapy, and if there is a suggestion of coercion in it, that can sometimes mess things up.

Brief therapy is therapy that is focused on clear, achievable goals. Therapy becomes like going to your family physician. You go to your doctor when you are hurting or worried about your physical health, and he or she treats you (usually in one or two visits) for what you came in for. If it works, you don't go back for more visits. You also choose your doctor carefully and then hope he or she is respectful, and knows how to listen, and is good at solving your medical problems, and doesn't mess you up worse with his or her treatment. The relationship, if any, develops through the treatment. You don't spend precious time (and money) working out your relationship with your doctor. The same is true with possibility therapy. And, like with your physician, you might come back to therapy at a later time because the problem you came for initially reoccurred or you have developed a new problem. Most of the time, after a few questions to rule out something fatal or serious, the doctor just proceeds to treat this new medical problem as a separate one. If you come in with a broken arm, your doctor X-rays and sets it. If the next year, you came in with a broken leg, the doctor X-rays the leg, sets it and sends you on your way, without necessarily relating it to your previous injury, except, for example, to rule out bone degeneration or domestic violence as causes. Likewise, sometimes therapy becomes serial brief therapy. New issues may be treated as separate, or as evidence that our previous interventions didn't work or last.

How often?

We don't always see people weekly. Sometimes we see them at first for several weeks or days in a row, and then as they are doing well, we stretch the length between sessions into weeks or months. As long as they are on track, we keep stretching the length, or terminate treatment altogether. How do we determine this spacing? By giving clients multiple choice options and letting them indicate, usually. We say, "Do you think we did what we needed to do, or would you like to come back? If you'd like to come back, is your sense that a month, or a week, or several weeks, or several months would be about right for the timing of our next meeting? We like to give a bit of time for the changes to happen, but you let us know what seems right to you."

With that, many clients choose weeks as their preferred spacing. We will sometimes have a sense of things different from the clients, and usually will say what we think the spacing should be after they give their preference. Especially if there has been some behaviour or concern about harm (suicide, homicide, domestic violence, severe drug or alcohol abuse), we will ask for continued meetings over the course of several years, but there will be considerable length of time between meetings if things seem to be going well.

Possibility therapy isn't always brief. Each person is an individual and there's no telling how long each person's treatment will last. We start therapy with the assumption that it will be brief and effective, but sometimes people teach us that it is not brief or effective. And darn if we don't listen! Sometimes we have learned that it was a good idea to take a longer time and more sessions. Sometimes it is a bad idea. The person (either client or therapist!) may become dependent on therapy, and it becomes a disempowering process. They and we may get distracted from a clear focus and don't get results. Of course, sometimes that's exactly what is needed, to get away from the pressure of having to get results. But be careful not to bullshit yourself. Long-term therapy *per se* is not necessarily better. What's better is what is respectful and effective.

Who is the expert: The client or the therapist?

We don't agree with approaches that claim that the client is the expert in the therapy process and the therapist should only be an interested, caring listener. In possibility therapy, we do see clients as the experts in their own lives, on what is bothering them, and how they want their lives to be when therapy is successful. And they are the experts on their own values. Possibility therapists don't claim any special knowledge about what is the right or healthy way to live. Just look at how perfect the life and family of any therapist you know are and you'll realize we suffer from the same problems everyone else does! So we don't try to tell clients the right way to live, or the correct values to hold.

However, we do consider ourselves experts in the change process, and see this important expertise as the reason clients come to us. So we are quite happy to take charge, give advice when it is asked for, or seems warranted, and we're also quite happy to just listen to our clients when they are on a roll, or just need to be listened to.

Oops - my karma just ran over your dogma: This book ain't the gospel truth!

There are as many therapeutic sects today as there are charismatic therapists to lead them. So why should you follow the O'Hanlon line? You shouldn't! Bill doesn't. Sandy doesn't either. Get to know some of the exciting therapists who are working right now - Lynn Hoffman, Peggy Penn, Michael White, David Epston, Karl Tomm, Steve Gilligan, Ben Furman, and Tapi Ahola, as well as Bill O'Hanlon. Read Milton Erickson and Jay Haley. Keep your eyes open. Read the *Family Therapy Networker, The Journal of Systemic Therapies,* and *Family Therapy Case Studies.*   Go with what is compassionate and respectful, and what works.

And remember, no matter how typical or stuck or hopeless a client may seem,

everybody is an exception!

Gratuitous jokes

Feel free to send us your own contributions for future editions

How many possibility therapists does it take to change a light bulb?
Maybe one, maybe three, maybe a friend can help, maybe it's bright enough in here already.

How many brief therapists does it take to change a light bulb?
Next joke, please.
But really, how many brief therapists does it take to change a light bulb?
I don't know, but they can do it in a flash.

How many Ericksonians does it take to change a light bulb?
That reminds me of when I was in school ...

How many hypnotists does it take to change a light bulb?
I don't know, they don't know, you are starting to feel dimmer and dimmer ...

How many pathology-focused therapists does it take to change a light bulb?
Light bulbs are unchangeable.

How many light bulbs does it take to change a psychotherapist?

The authors–in context

Photo by Sandy J. Beadle

Bill in a conference center.

Photo by Bill Kuhn

Sandy in a cedar swamp

About the authors

Bill: I play guitar, write songs, do marriage and family life, do psychotherapy, teach people how to do therapy, and write books. I'm a deviant, and proud of it.

Sandy: I'm interested in how people think and learn, and I'll be getting my MS before Lake Michigan freezes over. I like northern pine forests, PowerBooks, lakeshores, cedar swamps, creeks, and bogs, functional neuroanatomy, graphic design, fish, writing, walking, strange new music, and my wild assortment of warm, big-minded friends. Deviant and proud!

Brief Therapy Books 2000

Introducing Narrative Therapy:
A collection of practice-based writings

Cheryl White & David Denborough eds.   £16.50

Provides an introduction to narrative ideas and ways of working. Gathered together are a diversity of accessible, engaging, practice-based papers which all received enthusiastic feedback when first published. If you are a therapist, community worker or anybody else who want to understand more about narrative therapy and the different ways in which people are exploring and experimenting with narrative ways or working, then this book is for you.

NEW BOOK – JAN 2000

Extending Narrative Therapy:
A collection of practice-based papers   £17.50

This is an excellent collection of short, practical and readable essays on 'how to do' narrative therapy. It includes detailed descriptions of groupwork, work with survivors of abuse, community work, fighting racism, domestic violence and many other applications of narrative principles. It is light on jargon and rich with descriptions of effective work. What makes it especially appealing is that many of the contributors are first-time authors describing work in progress – none of which is beyond the reader's reach. It is an inspiring book and especially a book to read for inspiration about tomorrow.

'Catching Up' With David Epston:
A Collection of Narrative Practice-based Papers   £16.50

Ever wanted to catch up with David Epston and talk through the most significant aspects of his work over the last six years? If so, this inspiring and thoughtful collection of practice-based papers is for you! The papers trace the influences in David's recent work and explore in detail his therapeutic consultations. Specific sections address internalising/externalising, letter writing and his approach with anorexia/bulimia.

STILL AVAILABLE: Collected Papers volume I David Epston   £10

Five years of therapeutic cases, written from a personal rather than an objective and scientific viewpoint, and self-consciously concerned with the problems of representation in writing.

Narratives of Therapists' Lives

Michael White   £18

Thin conclusions? Vulnerable to fatigue and despair? In this book alternative views of the therapeutic relationship are explored. New options are expressed in a variety of forms, including "re-membering" conversations, "taking it back" practices, and "co-research" activities. In generating rich examples from work and from life, these practices provide an antidote to thin conclusions and are a source of sustenance and inspiration for the therapist.

Pickpockets on a Nudist Camp
Ben Furman & Tapani Ahola
£15.50

Towards a simplification of philosophical discourse surrounding family therapy, taking account of the effect of the observer, and the tyranny of language: "The point is in challenging our way of making sense of what's happening out there."

Bedtime Stories for Tired Therapists
ed. Leela Anderson
£15

A collection of inspiring and moving accounts of therapists' personal journeys, reflecting on the questions 'Given the emotional demands of this profession, why do we stay? How does the work challenge and change us, our thinking, our beliefs and our ways of seeing the world?

Re-authoring Lives: Interviews & Essays
Michael White
£15.50

This book makes compelling reading for counsellors, therapists and anyone who is interested in important questions about how people live their lives. You will especially appreciate this book if you are looking for hope and new visions in your work with people who are considered to have chronic problems; are developing ideas for consulting with people who have survived abuse; and if you want to work collaboratively with others in the generation of new possibilities in their lives.

Once Upon a Time
Narrative Therapy with Children and their Families
Edited by Alice Morgan
£16.50

This inspiring and accessible practice-based book explores how narrative therapy approaches can inform work with children and their families. Within it a range of narrative therapists relate the stories and ideas which they find most helpful in their practice. These are moving accounts of how children and their families reclaim their lives. This book will appeal to a wide range of counsellors, teachers, health professionals and others working and/or living with children.

Invitations to Responsibility –
The therapeutic engagement of men who are violent and abusive
Alan Jenkins
£15.50

Developing models of intervention that assist abusive males, by helping them to accept responsibility for their actions, to cease abusive behaviours, and relate respectfully to others.

The Personal is the Professional
Ed. Cheryl White & Jane Hales
£17

The experience of reading this collection of fascinating, moving and highly personal narratives is like attending a particularly intense workshop. The perspective offered is one which challenges oppressive interpretations which are common currency such as mother blaming, glorifying biological parenthood or sanctifying the nuclear family. This is a timely book for all therapists drawn to collaborative and transparent ways of working with clients. It is also "unputdownable".

BT Press, 17 Avenue Mansions, Finchley Road, London NW3 7AX. Cheques payable to 'BT Press' (+ 90p p&p per book)

Experience, Contradiction, Narrative & Imagination
Epston & White £15
A wide-ranging collaboration, covering such subjects as ways of addressing guilt, childhood stealing, dying with AIDS, and self-specialisation.

Narrative Therapy and Community Work £17
This book represents the workshops, presentations and conversations that took place at the inaugural Dulwich Centre Publications' Narrative Therapy and Community Work Conference in Adelaide. From practice-based seminar papers, to hearing from the voices of young people, this collection contains a diversity of thoughtful and invigorating writings. Contributors include writers from Israel, Australia, New Zealand, North America and South Africa.

BT Press

NEW UK EDITION – MAY 2000
Beyond Trauma and Therapy: Steps to a More Joyous Life
Yvonne Dolan   (Previous title fo this book was: One Small Step)   £16.50
For all those survivors who wonder when they will finally feel good, the answer is now. One Small Step reminds us that living well is the best revenge and provides the knowledge and tools to fully embrace life. Organised into easy-to-follow sections, readers will find help in: Moving beyond survivorhood; Enjoying the gifts of the present; Creating a joyous future; Responding to life's challenges; How to start a small steps support group.

Problem to Solution – *Revised and expanded edition*
Evan George, Chris Iveson & Harvey Ratner, foreword by Steve de Shazer   £12.50
A new expanded edition of the classic introductory text to Brief Solution Focused Therapy. New sections in this revised version include updated theory and practice and a new case study. It shows how many apparently chronic problems can be quickly and effectively solved by using the client's own aptitudes and strengths. It is a clear description of the approach and its central interest in exceptions, and how they form the basis of each client's own solution.

It's Never Too Late to have a Happy Childhood: From Adversity to Resilience
Ben Furman   £12.50
Good news from Finland – at last a volume from the author of Pickpocket in a Nudist Camp. There is no such thing as a perfect childhood. Where circumstances are subverted, promises are broken, expectations are dashed the balance is lost. Here are stories selected from over 300 contributions showing how it is possible to win out.

Moved to Tears, Moved to Action
Jane Lethem   £10
The author draws on her experience of Solution Focused Brief Therapy with women and their children to look at case studies through the lens of gender. She illustrates the ways in which its conversational style, emphasis on revealing hidden strengths and potential for tackling social injustice makes Solution Focused Brief Therapy particularly valuable for women.

Searching for Strengths in Child Protection Assessment

Trish Mylan & Jane Lethem £10

This book is for carers and other professionals in child protection assessments who confront vulnerability, breakdown and failure. The authors provide strategies to help find assets and strengths.

Family Preservation – A Brief Therapy Workbook

Insoo Kim Berg, editor Evan George £13.50

The author's work will change practice and will open new solutions for child protection workers who have become dissatisfied with a monitoring role and who are searching for ways to develop co-operation with their clients as a basis for building safety for children. .

A Field Guide to PossibilityLand

Bill O'Hanlon & Sandy Beadle £10

Possibility Therapy offers a new, more action- and future-oriented approach; a way of encouraging both therapist and client to try out new ideas and new ways to experiment with what works for the client.

Solution Focused Thinking In Schools

John Rhodes and Yasmin Ajmal £10

How can we find 'Brief' solutions to problems like classroom disruption in schools? How are frustrated teachers to be helped toward a better future with difficult pupils? This book suggests some simple ideas and strategies for finding solutions that work in the context of school. The emphasis is on looking for solution patterns as a basis for rekindling hope and facilitating change. It derives from a perspective which prefers to focus on the present situation and a person's definable goals rather than picking over the past.

Crossing the Bridge:
Integrating Solution Focused Therapy into Clinical Practice

Susan Lee Tohn & Jordan A. Oshlag £12.50

Most clinicians attend training workshops because they **need** to learn about brief/focused treatment, not because they **want** to. The demand is clear, the tools have been presented; however the guidance for how to **integrate** the concepts is too often missing. When mental health practicioners attempt to integrate the Solution Focused model into their clinical settings they are frustrated not because the techniques are too difficult, but because the systems in which and the assumptions under which they work are not adapting at the same pace as their therapeutic practice. This book discusses the integrative process in detail..

BT Press, 17 Avenue Mansions, Finchley Road, London NW3 7AX. Cheques payable to 'BT Press' (+ 90p p&p per book)

Brief Therapy Books 2000

NEW BOOKS

Becoming Miracle Workers - Language and Meaning in Brief Therapy
Gale Miller   £16

Provides a detailed exploration of brief therapy, a postmodern treatment mode that treats client's "problems" as social constructions, while encouraging those seeking treatment to replace personal troubles (negative stories) with new problem-solving skills (positive stories). Based on twelve years of research and observation, Miller's book describes in practicable detail how this method is employed in the Northland Clinic.

The Thin Book of Appreciative Inquiry
Sue Annis Hammond   £9

This book is an introduction to Appreciative Inquiry, an exciting philosophy for change. The major assumption of Appreciative Inquiry is that in every organisation something works and change can be managed through the identification of what works, and the analysis of how to do more of what works especially in organisations.

Lessons from the Field: Applying Appreciative Inquiry
Edited by Sue Annis Hammond and Cathy Royal Ph.D.   £18

Now is the time for re-thinking human organisation and change. There is widespread and growing cynicism about the very idea of planned change – the authors of this book counter this with a message of hope. Each of their compelling case studies shows how Appreciative Inquiry affects work in progress and what the authors learned. Written in a straightforward style it has many examples to encourage your own experimentation.

Divorce Busting
Michele Weiner-Davis   £15

Michele Weiner-Davis offers straightfoward advice on staying together, outlines the common illusions of divorce as a solution, and debunks the myth that one's past holds the key to solving problems. Using Solution-Oriented Brief Therapy, she then presents proven marriage-enriching, divorce-prevention techniques based on a simple formula: doing more of what works and less of what doesn't. The focus is on finding solutions – now – for marital discord instead of analysing past problems. With detailed case histories that show the techniques at work.

BT Press, 17 Avenue Mansions, Finchley Road, London NW3 7AX. Cheques payable to 'BT Press' (+ 90p p&p per book)

Managing People in Professional Practices
Anne Radford
£15.50

Revealing case studies show why personnel issues must be incorporated into strategic planning, with techniques on harmonising the interests of professionals, managers and support staff so as to forge effective teams. This book will also help managers who have difficulty delegating, give insufficient attention to employee development or rely on clone recruitment and corridor communications. Radford sets out the options, enabling readers to choose policies precisely suited to their needs.

Handbook of Solution-Focused Brief Therapy
Scott Miller, Mark Hubble & Barry Hubble, eds.
£31.50

This large volume, the first of its kind in the field, is an invaluable resource for all who are interested in brief therapy. There are chapters on the theory of the approach as well as important examples of outcome research. There is a series of extremely helpful applications of the approach in areas as diverse as grief therapy, inpatient psychiatric treatment, mandated (i.e. statutory) clients, and supervision.

Clues – Investigating Solutions in Brief Therapy
Steve de Shazer
£16.50

Once therapist and client are focused on investigating solutions rather than problems, therapy inevitably becomes brief. Engaging cases, often with surprising twists, illustrate this practice-based theory of brief therapy with a wide range of complaints.

In Search of Solutions
William Hudson O'Hanlon & Michele Weiner-Davis
£17

Readers who join O'Hanlon and Weiner-Davis in their search for solutions will find themselves on a path leading towards greater competency and empowerment for both their clients and themselves.

Resolving Sexual Abuse
Solution-Focused Therapy and Ericksonian Hypnosis for Adult Survivors
Yvonne M. Dolan
£21.95

This book provides specific and practical techniques, derived from solution-focused therapy and Ericksonian hypnosis, for the treatment of adult survivors of sexual abuse. Clients are encouraged to trust themselves, to move at their own right pace, and to recognise and build on tiny signs of healing.

BT Press, 17 Avenue Mansions, Finchley Road, London NW3 7AX. Cheques payable to 'BT Press' (+ 90p p&p per book)

Solution Talk – Hosting Therapeutic Conversations

Ben Furman and Tapani Ahola £17

"This is a highly readable and clinically practical book which teaches by illustration rather than by theorizing. It should be of interest to many family therapists who, regardless of orientation, have been trying to get away from a pathology orientation in their work." – AFTA Newsletter

Keys to Solution in Brief Therapy

Steve de Shazer £16.50

This book presents an innovative and theoretically elegant approach to brief therapy based on systems theory, the work of Milton Erickson and the author's many years of experience working with families.

The Solution-Oriented Woman – Creating the Life You Want

Pat Hudson £14.95

This future-focused book will help all kinds of women struggling with difficult situations. Pat's voice has the warmth and authority of a good big sister. The advice is practical, commonsensical and crystal clear.

Rewriting Love Stories Brief Marital Therapy

Patricia and William Hudson O'Hanlon £10.95

In this radical departure from traditional marital therapy approaches, this well-known wife and husband team uses the power of validation and solution-oriented strategies to break marital deadlocks. Those of us willing to follow their lead are in secure hands.

The Miracle Method

Scott D. Miller & Insoo Kim Berg £8.95

A radically new approach to problem drinking. This is a very practical self-help book, also useful for professional helpers.

Solution Focused Child Protection
– towards a positive frame for social work practice

Trish Walsh £9

What does a solution focused approach have to offer in the 'real life' situations facing social workers? Is it possible to work toward clients' goals while holding statutory responsibilty? What are the implications for the wider network? Walsh outlines the development of solution focused therapy and the application of a solution focused perspective to social work. She reflects on the work of four colleagues who present their highly individual

BT Press, 17 Avenue Mansions, Finchley Road, London NW3 7AX. Cheques payable to 'BT Press' (+ 90p p&p per book)

experiences of using the solution focused approach when grappling with such issues as child protection, the threat of family breakdown and the apparent prejudice of the wider network against the possibility of clients changing.

Their individual voices are drawn together by Walsh's analysis of the contribution of solution focused ideas and practices to successful social work intervention. While all the contributors acknowledge and honour their specific context and culture, their experiences are of general relevance to anyone with an interest in extending these ideas beyond the confines of the therapeutic consulting room.

A Brief Guide to Brief Therapy
Brian Cade and William Hudson O'Hanlon   £18

"With brief therapy getting deserved interest, the time is ripe for an overview. Cade and O'Hanlon state that they 'decided to collaborate on a book that would summarize the main elements, the ideas, principles, attitudes and techniques associated with brief therapy.' Read this work and you'll be glad that they did, and you did." – John H. Weakland

Working with the Problem Drinker
– A Solution-Focused Approach
Insoo Kim Berg and Scott D. Miller   £19.50

"It's a miracle! Finally, a wellness-oriented book about alcohol abuse treatment that capitalizes on client strengths and resources and invites the client to identify the goals for treatment… this is an excellent practice-oriented book." – Journal of Family Psychotherapy

Putting Difference to Work
Steve de Shazer   £17

Here, for the first time in his books, de Shazer takes a break from the strong emphasis on describing "how to do therapy" – although there is plenty of this – to place his work and that of his colleagues at the Brief Family Therapy Center within an overall philosophical description. Departing from the thinking of most schools of therapy, de Shazer proposes a philosophical position, based on the work of Wittgenstein, Derrida, and others, that situates the solution-oriented model within the developing purview of post-structuralist thought.

Words Were Originally Magic
Steve de Shazer   £24

Starting with a quote from Freud, "Words were originally magic" de Shazer maintains that words have never lost their original magic and may, indeed, be more magical than Freud imagined. In spite of or because of this magic, therapist and client can do practical work. While challenging assumptions about change, de Shazer includes numerous transcripts to demonstrate the process of using magical words and even magical numbers in solution-focused therapy.

BT Press, 17 Avenue Mansions, Finchley Road, London NW3 7AX. Cheques payable to 'BT Press' (+ 90p p&p per book)